Contact:
Managing visits
to children looked after
away from home

Acknowledgements

BAAF would like to express its sincere thanks to Peg McCartt Hess, Kathleen Ohman Proch and the Child Welfare League of America for their kind permission to enable us to publish this UK edition of their book, *Family Visiting in Out-of-home Care: A Guide to Practice*.

We would also like to thank Margaret Bryer for her assistance in preparing this edition and for providing the Foreword.

Notes on the authors

Peg McCartt Hess, Ph.D., ACSW, is Associate Professor, Columbia University School of Social Work, New York, NY, USA. For a number of years she co-ordinated a collaborative project between the Indiana University School of Social Work and the Indiana State Department of Public Welfare, developing and delivering training for child care social workers, supervisors, and foster carers. Dr Hess has also provided direct services and supervised social work staff in several family and children's services agencies. She teaches primarily in the areas of social work practice and research.

Kathleen Ohman Proch, Ph.D., is Professor, Graduate School of Social Work, University of Denver, USA. Her research has focused on placement disruption, parental visiting of children in out-of-home care, and adoption. Her interest in these areas grew out of her experience as a protective services worker with the Illinois Department of Children and Family Services. Dr Proch teaches primarily in the areas of law and social welfare policy.

Contact:
Managing visits to children looked after away from home

Peg McCartt Hess
Kathleen Ohman Proch

B *ritish*

A *gencies*

for **A** *doption*

and **F** *ostering*

First published in the USA in 1988 by the
Child Welfare League of America as *Family
Visiting in Out-of-home Care: A Guide to
Practice*

© Child Welfare League of America 1988

This UK edition published by
British Agencies for Adoption & Fostering
(BAAF)
11 Southwark Street
London SE1 1RQ

© Foreword by Margaret Bryer 1993

**British Library Cataloguing in
Publication Data**
Hess, Peg McCartt
    Contact: Managing visits to children
    looked after away from home
    I. Title   II. Proch, Kathleen
    362.7

    ISBN 1-873868-12-X

Designed by Andrew Haig & Associates
Typeset, printed and bound by Russell Press
in Great Britain

Contents

Foreword

Family Visiting in Out-of-home Care: A Guide to Practice was published in 1988 by the Child Welfare League of America. Although written from the American viewpoint, it is wholly applicable to practice in the UK. This UK edition, titled *Contact: Managing visits to children looked after away from home*, essentially retains most of the original text, and changes in terminology and legal references have been made to render it more accessible to a UK readership. Readers will note that the term "child" has been used throughout to include both children and young people.

This Foreword sets the book in the context of UK practice, highlighting some aspects of contact that are of particular concern to many social workers. The legal context of the main text is England and Wales following the introduction of the Children Act 1989. There is a note on the Scottish legal context at the end of the Foreword. Studies familiar to readers in the UK have been cited in the text, and studies by the authors and other relevant literature are listed in Further Reading.

Since the introduction of the Children Act 1989 in England and Wales, with its emphasis on the importance of contact between children and their families of origin, social workers have been endeavouring to manage complex situations in which the needs and wishes of the various parties rarely coincide, and where the practical and emotional components are very demanding.

There is overwhelming evidence that for the majority of children and young persons being looked after in local authority care, some form of contact is beneficial.[1,2,3,4] The challenge is to identify the optimum pattern of contact for a given child and family and to develop strategies to achieve it. At the same time there must be adequate protection for those children for whom visits or other forms of contact are harmful.[5] Sometimes difficult choices have to be made when there are more relatives seeking contact with a child than the child can cope with, and it becomes necessary to identify those who will best meet the child's needs, now and in the future.

The issues are not new but they have been thrown into a stronger focus, not only by the Act, but also by a series of research studies which, over a number of years, have produced a remarkably consistent correlation between high levels of contact and the return of children to their families. At the same time they demonstrate the extremely low levels of contact of any sort which actually take place between separated children and their parents.[6,7,8,9,10] Similarly, decreasing contact is found in studies of families after divorce.[11] On a more positive note, a study in Northern Ireland and evidence from placements within black families indicate that in some communities family links are given higher priority.[12,13.]

Most research is concerned with face to face contact – visits between children and their families – and this is the focus of this book. The term 'contact' of course covers all manner of links from frequent visits to occasional phone calls, or exchange of news and photographs at Christmas. Many of the ideas given here about managing visits are applicable or adaptable to other forms of contact.

Contact: Managing visits to children looked after away from home concentrates on visits between children and their families when the plan is for the children to return home (the majority of placements). The focus is on those parents who are motivated and capable of co-operating in the return of their children. It reminds us to treat all parents as capable partners unless, or until, we have reason to believe that they are unable or unwilling to co-operate.[14,15]

Many of the children will be accommodated and, therefore, the parents can, in law, see their children whenever they like. It is imperative that local authorities do not abuse their authority by imposing conditions on parents of accommodated children. Parents have to be encouraged to co-operate in a reasonable plan that does not place undue strains on a child or the carers. Social workers and carers should also be alert to the many barriers to contact which mitigate against successful visiting, such as distance of placement from home, poor health, and other demands on the family and the carers.[16] It is self-evident that co-operative planning between the social worker, parents, carers and child or young person (if appropriate) will stand the best chance of success.

It is helpful to look at what each person wants, needs and can cope with, and check that plans are based first on the needs of the children rather than on what the adults can cope with or want. Such an exercise can be useful in sorting out priorities for visiting when many people are involved. For example, if the objective is rehabilitation of a child and the purpose of contact is to build up the relationship between mother and child and to improve parenting skills, then the wishes of other relatives for contact may not be met for a while because the child (and probably the carers) cannot cope with it.

When children are the subject of care orders because their parents have abused them, or failed to protect them, contact may have to be controlled, and in extreme cases terminated. The criteria on which such decisions are based are beyond the scope of this book, but the children still need links with their background, and it may be that social workers will feel encouraged by this book to leave the door ajar to the family rather than slamming it shut. Security need not always be equated with exclusivity. There is research evidence that children in long-term placement fare better if they have some regular contact with their family of origin, but that they do not do so well if the contact is irregular. Also, it is a sad fact that many placements do not work out, and that children are subjected to a fragmented sequence of moves. Contact with the birth family may provide the only continuity for the child. A significant number of young people do find their way back to their families, even after many years in care.[17,18]

For these reasons contact should only be terminated before a child is placed in a permanent substitute family if this is necessary to protect the child. Unfortunately, there is still evidence that some social workers apply for termination of contact because they think that it will be easier to place children who will not have visits from their parents. On the other hand, many children are now "drifting" in care while their social workers try to find carers who can manage appropriate contact.

The requirements of the Children Act in relation to contact has great implications for the recruitment, training, support and remuneration of foster carers. It is not surprising that workers feel overwhelmed by the size of the task and the feelings that contact may engender. A common way of coping is to impose controls and this may be one explanation for some worrying trends in current practice.

3

One trend is to set rigid contact plans which are not flexible enough to be responsive to the changing needs of the children and parents, or to the progress of the plan. The goal of work with every child (except young people heading for independent living) is to establish that child in a permanent family home where his or her priority needs can be met. For most children that permanence will be sought within the family of origin, and only if that cannot be achieved will permanent substitute family care become the plan. Whilst the objective may remain steady the planning required to achieve that objective will alter as children develop. The first contact plan should be made before the child is accommodated, and will be set out in the care plan. It will then be reassessed at each review. This book takes you through the stages of work towards reunification of children with their families, identifying the changing purposes of contact.

From the point of view of the social workers, carers, lawyers and other professionals, a timetable for contact seems more manageable and fair than a more flexible plan. Parents and children may be reassured by a clear structure. For short periods, such as the time leading to court proceedings, or other time-limited pieces of work, a precise plan may well be desirable. Yet timetables can be insensitive to the changing needs of children. A child may need to see a parent for a prolonged visit, or several times in quick succession. A meeting once a month may be spent by both child and parent trying to re-establish where they were the month before, and they may never have time to move forwards before the visit is over and the pattern is repeated. Social workers are constrained by decisions of courts when care orders or contact orders are made. However, the courts rely on information from the social workers and guardians *ad litem* about the needs and wishes of children and parents. In many instances social workers and lawyers could recommend to courts minimum and maximum amounts of contact. This would give a framework within which there could be flexibility. Parents and relatives might also be helped to see that, for example, three or four half-day visits per month could be more satisfying, and much easier to manage, than a rigid one-hourly visit each week.

There is another worrying trend. Some agencies opt for having contact visits in "a neutral place", such as a family centre, rather than in the foster home or parent's home, not just in those cases where this is essential to protect the child and foster carers but as a more general practice. The artificiality of visits may be compounded if they are held in a place where activities are restricted and the parents cannot fulfil any of the basic nurturing tasks of parenthood. In unseparated families, parents interact with their children while they are doing domestic jobs, or watching TV, or when they go out together. There will often be other people around. In contrast, parents and children on contact visits are put in an extraordinary position of great intensity, intimacy and stress. It is not surprising that they find it hard to cope and sometimes opt out.

People's behaviour under stress can be categorised broadly as approach, avoidance or ambivalence. Some parents and children predominantly show avoidance (withdrawal, rejection, depression), or approach (aggression, over-excitement, swamping with affection or sweets, and certain anti-social behaviours), but most show ambivalence, veering from one behaviour to another. Carers and social workers may feel ambivalent about contact and may not be consistent. Each person's behaviour reflects their attempt to solve a problem; in this instance the practicalities and feelings engendered by separation and contact. When parents and children (and carers and social workers) do not manage this very well we are quick to judge. It is hard to see distress as anything but negative, and it is tempting to reduce or end contact rather than try alternative strategies for improving it and making it more authentic.

This guide is all about strategies for managing contact, starting with the premise that for most children contact visits work best in the foster home or the parents' home. It gives a clear analysis of the steps involved in preparing for a visit, managing the visit and coping with the aftermath. The authors show a sympathetic understanding of the role and feelings of the children, parents, substitute carers and social workers. Above all, it forces us to focus on the purpose of contact at each stage of placement and to plan according to that purpose.

Some workers may find it unrealistic in its assumption of the availability of certain resources. For example, there is mention of parentcraft classes to teach parents the skills they lack. Such classes will not be found in many places in the UK. The authors assume that therapists and counsellors are available to parents, when the reality here is a desperate shortage of such professionals. But the book challenges us to look again at what resources are available, and to use more effectively the time and skills of those who are involved. We may need to reassess our judgements about supervision of visits, so that the fullest protection is given where needed, but also so that parents are left alone with their children if there is no reason to intervene.

Most importantly, this book is about attitudes: the commitment to the principle of contact visits, to action towards achieving them, and empathy with those involved. All the evidence adds up to show that if the attitudes are positive, successful contact appropriate to a child's needs can be managed.[19,20] However, if the attitudes of any one party are negative and obstructive, then the chances of good contact are instantly and seriously reduced. Here is the message that we have to spend time to save time; that planning and managing appropriate contact for children from the time that they are first looked after is the greatest contributory factor to the successful and speedy reunification of children with their families.

Margaret Bryer
September 1993

Note on the legal context in Scotland
Readers in Scotland will be aware that the Scottish legal system is different from that in England and Wales and that social workers need to bear in mind the different structures of legal procedures in that jurisdiction. In particular, heed needs to be taken of the system of Children's Hearings in Scotland and the various orders which can be made in the Sheriff Court.

Particular points to bear in mind include the following:
The sharp distinction between children "accommodated" and children subject to care orders in the English legislation, where parental responsibility remains with the parents of children who are accommodated and is transferred to the local authority where a care order is in force, is not a feature of Scottish legal arrangements. Where a child is subject to a supervision requirement from a Children's Hearing, parental rights remain with the parents and questions of access which are in dispute may require to be resolved by the Children's Hearing. The assumption

of parental rights by a local authority in Scotland is a separate process under s16 of the Social Work (Scotland) Act 1968 which has its own procedure for dealing with appeals and determination of questions of access where there is a dispute between the parents and the local authority. Since the Children Act 1989, the terms "looked after" and "accommodated" have acquired in England and Wales a specific statutory gloss which overlays the ordinary meaning of the terms and readers need to be aware that the statutory meaning is of no significance in Scotland. The core of the requirement for the local authority to make care plans for children is contained in the welfare and review provision in s20 of the Social Work (Scotland) Act 1968. There are specific requirements in the Boarding Out and Fostering of Children (Scotland) Regulations 1985. Some of these mirror requirements in the Children Act in England & Wales, e.g. Regulation 16 which requires the care authority to consider when making arrangements for two or more children in the same family either to ensure the children are fostered in the same home or, where that is not appropriate or practicable, in homes as near together as is appropriate or practicable.

This book is not a book about legal procedures. Therefore, rather than overburden the text with cross-references to Scottish procedure which would necessarily be quite extensive in some cases because concepts and criteria would require explanation, we have formed the view that Scottish readers will be able to note in the text references to the Children Act and realise that these require to be translated or considered in terms of prevailing Scottish legislation and put in hand the necessary enquiries on their own behalf.

Alison J Newman and Donal Giltinan

References

1 DoH, *Patterns and Outcomes in Child Placement: Messages from current research and their implications*, HMSO, 1991

2 Family Rights Group, *Fostering Parental Contact: Arguments in favour of preserving contact between children in care and their families*, FRG, 1982

3 Farmer E, Parker R, *Trials and Tribulations: Returning children from local*

authority care to their families, HMSO, 1991

4 Fratter J, *Family Placement and Access*, Barnardo's, 1989

5 O'Hara M, 'Access Visits that Betray an Abused Child's Trust', *Childright*, October 1990

6 Aldgate J, 'Identification of Factors Influencing Children's Length of Stay in Care', in *New Developments in Foster Care and Adoption*, Routledge & Kegan Paul, 1980

7 Holloway V, 'Making Contact', *Foster Care*, March 1992

8 Packman J with Randall J Jacques, *Who Needs Care*, Blackwell, 1986

9 DHSS, *Social Work Decisions in Child Care: Recent Research Findings and their Implications*, HMSO, 1985

10 See 1 above

11 Wallerstein and Kelly, *Surviving the Break up*, Grant McIntyre, 1980

12 Kelly G, *Patterns of Care: Child care carers and patterns that shape them*, Department of Social Studies, The Queen's University, Belfast, 1990

13 Charles M, Rashid S, Thoburn J, 'The Placement of Black Children in Permanent New Families', *Adoption & Fostering*, Vol 16 (3), 1992

14 Aldgate J, 'Partnership with Parents: Fantasy and Reality', *Adoption & Fostering*, Vol 15 (2), 1991

15 Fisher M, Marsh P, Phillips D with Sainsbury E, *In and Out of Care*, BAAF/Batsford, 1986

16 Millham S, Bullock R, Hosie K and Haak M, *Lost in Care, The Problems of Maintaining Links between Children in Care and their Families*, Aldershot-Gower, 1986

17 See 3 above

18 Stein M and Carey K, *Leaving Care*, Blackwell, 1986

19 See 15 above

20 Jenkins S and Norman E, *Filial Deprivation and Foster Care*, Columbia University Press, 1972, USA

Introduction

Imagine that you have just become a social worker to two children placed this week because they were abused by their parents. If the children are comfortable enough to ask, their first question to you is likely to be, 'When can we see our parents?' This is just one of many questions concerning visiting that you will have to answer in placement. How often will visits be arranged? How long will they be? Where will they be held? Will they be supervised? How will the visiting plan change over time? The list of questions is long, and each decision is difficult, requiring careful assessment of risk to children and of parents' abilities to care for their children.

Contact: Managing visits to children looked after away from home will help you answer these questions as you develop and carry out visiting plans. Visits are at the heart of permanency planning. Although published research supports the importance of visiting, few resources have been available to assist those who develop and implement visiting plans that facilitate achievement of case work and in doing so, decrease the length of time children spend in foster care.

Planning visits and making them meaningful for children and their parents are demanding and time-consuming tasks, but they are critically important to families and to case outcomes. Our hope is that this resource will not only guide your work with families, but will also encourage you in your commitment to maintaining relationships between children and their parents.

Contact: Managing visits to children looked after away from home begins by discussing the importance and purposes of visiting and by identifying the ways in which agency policies and placement practices encourage or constrain visiting. The second chapter introduces the concept of visiting as an essential component of agency service. It outlines the elements of the visiting plan and, recognising that most children being looked after will return home, describes the changes in visiting plans that should typically occur as the time for reunification nears. The subsequent three chapters provide guidelines for considering factors related to children, their parents, and their substitute carers in developing visiting plans. These chapters focus on the individual assessments that must continually be made in each case in order to develop a sound visiting plan. The sixth chapter offers suggestions for preparing participants for visits and for evaluating and documenting visits. The book concludes with a discussion of the demands visiting imposes on workers and ways in which you can relieve some of the stress you encounter.

Throughout the book we have used the inclusive term 'substitute carer'. Children may be placed with a foster family, a relative, or in a residential establishment. Although the process for planning visits and the role of the carer in visits may vary somewhat depending on the nature of the placement, the same guidelines for decision making concerning visits apply.

Contact: Managing visits to children looked after away from home shares what we have learned from our research, from our own practice experiences, and from the experiences of our colleagues. Throughout the discussion we have asserted standards for practice, recognising the realities that complicate your ability to achieve that standard in each case.

We are gratful to the following people for their assistance with this book. Several colleagues read and provided very useful comments on an earlier draft: Janet Deland, Jeanne Howard, Eve Krasinski, Carol Massat, Edie Olson, and Anita Osborn. Jane Winters cheerfully and ably typed the multiple drafts. We are particularly grateful to Carl Schoenberg of the Child Welfare League of America for his encouragement and for his wisdom and editorial skill.

Peg McCartt Hess
Kathleen Ohman Proch

1 Visiting in context

Although contact between children in placement and their families may sometimes seem simply a legal requirement, visiting is critical to a child's well-being and to successful reunification of the family. Arranging visits and making them meaningful are two of the most important aspects of work with children in placement. This chapter discusses the importance and purposes of visiting, and it identifies the ways in which agency policies and resources support or constrain visiting. It provides information that you can use to encourage a child's parents to visit and to encourage a child's substitute carers to facilitate visiting. It also offers a background against which you can examine your own perceptions of visiting and your agency's policies concerning visiting.

Why is visiting important?

Available research suggests that visiting is important for two reasons. First, the psychological well-being and developmental progress of children in placement are enhanced by contact with their parents.[1,2,3] Second, children who are visited frequently by their parents are more likely to be returned to their parents' care than are children who are visited infrequently.[4,5]

Perhaps more important than these conclusions of research is the realisation that children who are in placement are like all other children in being attached to their parents and to other members of their families. Children in placement miss their families when they are apart, and they miss their homes when they are away. Visiting, then, is important simply because it allows children to be with the people to whom they are attached, and if possible, to be in the homes they remember. Managing contact well is more than a casework tool; it is an expression of your caring for children. While visiting between children and their parents is the focus of most contact planning and most of this book, visiting between children and other members of their families is also important. Siblings, grandparents, and other relatives are all part of the world from which children in placement have been uprooted.

What are the specific purposes of visiting?

While recognising the value of visiting in and of itself, visiting can and should also be thought of as a planned intervention. This further justifies the development of visiting plans and the use of agency resources to support visiting. What are some of the purposes of visiting that make it an integral part of services to children in placement?

Maintaining relationships

The primary purpose of visiting is to allow children to preserve relationships with people who are important to them. This purpose supercedes all other purposes of visiting. It justifies visiting not only between parents and children, but also between siblings who are separated in placement, between children and members of their extended families, and in some cases, between children and foster carers who cared for them earlier. The child's need for continuity of relationships and the importance of visiting to continuity must be respected, even though visiting is also used for other purposes that are suggested below.

Although preservation of family relationships between children and parents and between siblings separated in placement is obviously essential to successful reunification, it is also important if the plan is not reunification. In many cases children will and should remain attached to siblings and members of the extended family even when they will not return to parental care. These family members, like former substitute carers, may be important resources for children both while they are being looked after and when they reach adulthood. Strong relationships can only be maintained through frequent visiting.[6]

Reassurance

Visiting reassures children that they have not been abandoned, a common and psychologically damaging fear of children in placement. Visiting reassures parents that the agency wants the family to be unified again and is not trying to separate them from their children. Visiting also reassures children and other family members that everyone in the family is well, freeing them from unnecessary worry and releasing more energy to devote to developmental tasks or other goals. If a family member is ill then the child can be helped to accept and understand the illness and its implications without unreal anxieties or fantasies.

Assessment

Visiting allows social workers to observe interactions between parents and children. This is a necessary prerequisite to developing the care plan, evaluating progress in meeting objectives of care, modifying the treatment plan, and determining if or when a child can return home. It may also provide an opportunity for social workers to assess parental motivation and capacity. Are the parents willing to co-operate in establishing a visiting plan? Can they arrange their own transport to the visit or to pick up their child for the visit? Do they keep scheduled appointments? Can they plan appropriate activities for their children? Can they care for and protect their children during visits?

One major qualification must be added. Although the answers to questions concerning motivation and capacity are important, perhaps essential, indicators of the probability of successful reunification, they must not be influenced by barriers to visiting that might emanate from the agency. For example, some agency requirements regarding the parents' responsibilities when visiting may be impracticable, and if this is the case, a parent's failure to meet them must not be interpreted as lack of interest in his or her child.

Improving parenting skills

In many cases, treatment involves teaching skills to parents. During visits, social workers, family aides, therapists, and children's foster carers can teach child care and demonstrate ways of setting and enforcing limits. The visit then becomes an integral and active part of treatment. Even when parenting skills are not being taught during the visits themselves, visits remain an important part of treatment. Visits provide an opportunity for parents to test and to improve the skills they might be learning in parenting classes or counselling sessions. Moreover, in cases where the relationship between parents and children is troubled, visits allow family members to develop better ways of interacting and communicating. And when parents and children are strongly attached, the prospect of more frequent and longer visits can be a powerful motivator to remain engaged in treatment.

Treatment necessarily involves confronting reality. Parents need to experience what child care and supervision really involve. Some parents need to decide whether they really want to be a parent. Some children need to confront the reality that their parents will never be able to care adequately for them and they may not be able to return home. Older children, if they are to return home, may have to assume more responsibility for their own care and protection. In some cases, parents need to acknowledge that their children are unwilling to return home and would undermine attempts to reunite the family. These realities can best be confronted – and perhaps can only be confronted – through visiting. Without visiting, abilities and desires are abstract and therefore unclear. In the absence of contact, it is easy for both parents and children to fantasise and to deny reality. Parents and children must experience being together to be able to determine for themselves if reunification is possible. Moreover, when reunification is not possible, it is easier for family members to accept that fact if it has been tested through extensive visiting.

Documentation

Recommendations either for return home or for alternative permanent substitute care must be carefully justified. Recording of not only the visiting plan, but also events that occur surrounding and during visits, can support recommendations that you make. On the one hand, for example, if a parent who has been involved in visit planning and has agreed to a written visiting plan repeatedly fails without just cause to visit, then there is reinforcement for reduction or termination of contact. On the other hand, if it can be shown that there was no evidence of abuse during visits that progressed from short visits in the office to visits overnight at home, then there is added support for return home.

Conditions that facilitate visiting

If visiting is to occur frequently and to be a significant component of service to families, certain conditions must be met. Some of these conditions are within your control; they concern your attitudes and the decisions you make. Others are not within your immediate control; these relate to your agency's policies and resources. An awareness of all these conditions, however, may help in understanding the limits of what can be achieved and may encourage you to seek changes in the policies and practices followed in your agency.[7]

Social workers must be committed to visiting
Arranging and supporting visits are two of the most difficult and time-consuming aspects of social workers' work with children in placement. Visits can place enormous stress on you. You worry about children being physically or emotionally harmed during visits. You watch some children approach their parents during visits, only to be rejected or ignored. You try to comfort children when their parents fail to visit. You see the pain of goodbyes and of parents' and children's attempts to reassure each other. You spend seemingly endless hours arranging a visit and co-ordinating transport only to have a parent or foster carer cancel the visit at the last minute. Scheduling visits, especially for holidays and on children's birthdays, often seems to be a thankless task.

It is difficult for social workers to maintain their commitment to visiting in the face of the demands it imposes, but commitment is essential because the social worker is pivotal in the case. Your commitment will influence parents, children, and other service providers. In many cases, your commitment to visiting may determine whether successful reunification occurs.

Social workers must have empathy for parents
It is easy to create barriers to visiting: to arrange visits at the office and only during regular business hours, to expect parents with no income or limited income to arrange their own transport, and to view every missed visit as a sign of the parent's lack of caring or interest. In reality, visiting is extremely difficult for parents. It stirs their feelings of missing their children. It reminds them of their failures and inadequacies. Each visit tells parents that while they are not capable of caring for their children, someone else is. If the opportunity to visit is to be more than a test of

parents' interest in their children, and perhaps an unreasonable test at that, visits must be planned with parents' needs and resources in mind.[8]

Carers must be committed to visiting
Visiting does not depend only on the social worker, the child, and the child's parents. Visiting also depends on the child's carers, who can either support or undermine the visiting plan.[9]

Foster carers and residential workers play important roles in visiting. They can help prepare a child for a visit. They can comfort and reassure a child or respond in other ways that are helpful to a child following a visit. They can transport the child to and from visits. Foster carers can allow visits in their own homes and be actively involved in visits, modelling healthy parent-child interactions and teaching child care.

But carers may be unco-operative in arranging visits and reluctant to assist with transport. They can show their dislike and distrust of a child's parents through words and actions. They can refuse to accept that a child's negative behaviour or withdrawal following visits indicate healthy attachment and distress over separation, and instead insist that visits occur less frequently in order to minimise the problems with which they must contend. Because of their ability to influence the child and the implementation of the agency plan, the willingness of substitute carers to facilitate visiting is critical.

Concerns about carers include not only your agency's foster carers or residential workers, but also the policies and practices of other agencies from which your agency may purchase services. In a survey of the policies of voluntary agencies, we found that some residential treatment facilities made the frequency and the place of visits dependent on the child's behaviour. Some agencies had policies prohibiting visits in the child's foster home. Policies of this kind may seem justified from the agencies' viewpoint, but they may result in strong resistance to plans you develop. In such instances, you may be required to enlist the support of your supervisor and your agency's administration to enforce your visiting plan.

Foster carers must not be overburdened
The difficulty of recruiting foster carers goes without saying, especially carers who are committed to reunification and to strengthening children's

relationships with their families. It is easy to overuse such foster carers by asking that they take just one more child or that they take a child for whom they are reluctant to care, either because the child has special needs or because the child appears not to fit well with children already in the home. But by asking foster carers to care for too many children from different families or to care for too many children with special needs (subject to the limits set by the Children Act), we almost assure that visiting will become problematic, no matter how committed the foster carer is to visiting. Just as visiting places emotional demands on social workers and requires a significant amount of their time, it is emotionally demanding and time-consuming for foster carers. They simply do not have the emotional resources or the time to prepare many children for visits and respond helpfully to the children following visits. Similarly, if there are several children in the home, the foster carers cannot be as helpful in providing transport for one child because they do not have the time, and they cannot be as flexible in scheduling. They must balance the need to care for the child who has the visit today with the need to care for other children in the home.

Children must be placed near their parents' homes
The Children Act 1989 requires that children be placed in the most family-like setting available and in close proximity to the parents' home, consistent with the best interests and special needs of the child. The extent to which this requirement is met has a direct impact on visiting.

Visits may be easier to arrange when children are living in foster homes than when they are living in residential care. In foster family care, you and the parent need only plan with the foster carers, taking into account only the child's, the parents and the foster carers' schedules. If children are in residential care, however, planning visits must often take into account not only the child's needs and activities, but also those of the entire establishment. Moreover, if the child is in residential care, it may be more difficult to find a venue for the visit that offers privacy and an opportunity for natural interaction.

Even more important to planning visits than the type of placement is the nearness of the placement to the parents' home. The closer parents and children are geographically, the more frequently they can visit. This occurs for two reasons. First, it is reasonable to expect parents to visit more often and arrange their own transport if they have less far to travel. Second, if children and parents are located near each other, you and others do not need to spend as much time and money transporting them.

Siblings must be placed together

It is also a requirement of the Children Act that siblings be placed together whenever possible. Siblings who are separated in placement suffer greater loss and disruption of family life than do siblings who are not separated. They lose not only their parents, but also their brothers and sisters. Siblings who are placed together can offer each other support and reassurance. Moreover, if siblings are separated, reunification requires not only a reconstruction of parent-child relationships, but also reconstruction of sibling relationships.[10]

The placement of siblings also influences visiting. If siblings are separated, visit planning becomes more complex. For example, consider a case in which three children are placed in separate foster homes and in which the goal for all three children is to return home. You must decide whether the parents are going to visit all the children at once, or whether they are going to visit the children individually. On the one hand, if parents are to visit all three children together, you must co-ordinate the carers' schedule with the schedules of the three children and their foster carers and perhaps with your schedule. The times when visits are convenient for all four households are likely to be few. On the other hand, if the parents visit the children individually, the time and cost spent in visiting becomes a significant consideration, not only for the parents, but also for you and for others providing supervision or transport. Moreover, if the children are not together for visits with their parents, then you must arrange times for the children to visit each other.

The requirement of written plans for contact

Policy requiring written plans for contact appears to be an important prerequisite to frequent visiting and eventual reunification and is now a requirement of all agencies under the Children Act Regulations. Researchers have found that the more frequently parents visit, the higher the probability of reunification.[11,12,13] We have found that care plans specify visiting in accord with agency policy and that parents visit in accordance with care plans. If there is no schedule for visits, parents do not visit. But if there is a schedule, parents keep it, especially if they were involved in making the schedule.

Policy articulates a preference as to what should occur. But more importantly, if policy specifies a given minimum visiting frequency, agency resources should support the policy. In addition, policy gives social workers some authority or leverage in working with substitute carers who are reluctant to support frequent visits.

The importance of specific written plans cannot be overstated. First, specific written visiting plans can prevent misunderstandings by clearly stating expectations and schedules. Second, specific and written plans, developed with the input of all parties involved in visiting, serve as contracts. Compliance with a realistic contract can be used to support recommendations either to return children home or to terminate parental contact.

Agency resources which promote visiting

Agency resources have a profound effect on visiting. Visiting can occur only infrequently in the absence of resources to support it. What resources influence visiting?[14,15,16]

Low and varied case loads. Visiting is time-consuming for social workers. One visit, whether it is to be supervised or unsupervised, can easily take an entire afternoon. Moreover, if visiting is to be an integral part of services, time is needed to plan the visit and its objectives, to prepare the parents and the child for it, and to discuss it with the parents and child after it has occurred. You also need time to discuss the visit with the child's foster carers after it has occurred, alerting them to any special needs the child might have, and noting any observations you would like them to make. You need time to record what occurred during the visit and how the participants reacted to it.

The demands visiting imposes on social workers' time must be considered in case allocation. If visiting is to occur frequently and to be used creatively, the number of cases in a case load in which reunification is the goal or in which frequent visiting is to be encouraged for other reasons must be low. The higher the case load, and the greater the number of cases in which reunification is the goal, the less frequent the visiting is likely to be. When case loads are high, visiting is also less likely to be a meaningful part of the care plan.

Placement resources. The frequency of visiting depends on the geographic distance between the parents and the child, the extent to which siblings are separated, and the commitment and resources of carers. All of these factors relate to the quantity and quality of placement resources available to the agency. Visiting can occur frequently and be used creatively in concert with care goals only when the agency has placement resources that allow children to be placed together near their parents and with carers who are committed to visiting.

Flexible hours. If visits are to meet the needs of parents and children, they may need to be arranged outside standard office hours. Instead, they should occur at weekends, in the evenings, and over holidays. Visiting will be supported by agency policy allowing flexitime or compensation for work outside normal office hours. Similarly, visiting will be supported if the agency has regular scheduled working hours at times convenient for parents, for example, evening and weekend hours.

Private and comfortable visiting rooms. Visits often cannot or should not occur in the parents' home, primarily because of concerns over the child's safety. At times visiting in the foster home may not be advisable. However, visits should be held at a venue that allows for privacy and natural interaction. In order to use visits at least in part for assessment, they need to be held where the visit can be unobtrusively observed. For these reasons, the various purposes of visiting can best be achieved if the agency has well-equipped, comfortable visiting rooms, ideally with one-way mirrors.

Volunteers and others to assist with visiting. Volunteers, family aides, therapists, and other professionals can be very helpful in visiting, easing the demands placed on social workers. Volunteers and others can transport children and parents to visits and, in some instances, supervise visits. Simply put, agencies with committed volunteers can offer more visiting than agencies without volunteers, and agencies who can pay staff members other than social workers to assist with visiting can organise more frequent visits.

Financial assistance for parents. An aspect of visiting that may be overlooked is its cost to parents. If a visit is not at their home, the parents may have to pay for transport and for the care of children who are at home. If the visit is at their home, the parents need to buy extra food and pay other costs of caring for the child. Although none of these costs are extreme, they can be significant to a parent on a very low income or dependent on welfare benefits. If the agency is to expect or encourage frequent visits or extended home visits, it must have some way to assist parents with the costs of visiting when necessary.

References

1   Family Rights Group, *Fostering Parental Contact: Arguments in favour of preserving contact between children in care and their families*, FRG, 1982

2   Family Rights Group, *Promoting Links: Keeping children and families in touch*, FRG, 1986

3   Triseliotis J, 'Foster Care Outcome: Review of key research findings', *Adoption & Fostering* Vol 13 (3), 1989

4   Aldgate J, 'Identification of Factors Influencing Children's Length of Stay in Care', in *New Developments in Foster Care and Adoption*, Routledge & Kegan Paul, 1980

5   Fratter J, *Family Placement and Access*, Barnardo's, 1989

6   Wedge P and Mantle G, *Sibling Groups and Social Work*, Avebury Gower, 1991

7   Gibson P and Parsloe P, 'What Stops Access to Children in Care', *Adoption & Fostering* Vol 8 (1), 1984

8   Millham S, Bullock R, Hosie K and Haak M, *Lost in Care: The problems of maintaining links between children in care and their families*, Aldershot-Gower, 1986

9   Waterhouse S, 'How Foster Carers View Contact', *Adoption & Fostering* Vol 16 (2), 1992

10 See 6 above

11 Aldgate J, 'Partnership with Parents: Fantasy and Reality', *Adoption & Fostering* Vol 15 (2), 1991

12 Fisher M, Marsh P, Phillips D with Sainsbury E, *In and Out of Care*, BAAF/Batsford, 1986

13 See 8 above

14 DoH, *Patterns and Outcomes in Child Placement: Messages from current research and their implications*, HMSO, 1991

15 Farmer E and Parker R, *Trials and Tribulations: Returning children from local authority care to their families*, HMSO, 1991

16 See 12 above

2 Contact as a component of the care plan

The visiting plan is part of the contact plan which itself is an essential component of the care plan. The visiting plan is based in part on the permanency goal for the child, and therefore should help achieve the goal and reflect progress towards it.

Because most children in placement should and will return home, visiting in most cases will be used to support the goal of reunification. But even when return home is not the goal, visiting will often continue to play a role in the care plan.

Planning assumptions

The discussion on planning in this chapter is based on several assumptions.

The agency is required to develop plans

Care planning is the responsibility of the agency, in consultation with the parents. The balance of responsibility will vary according to whether a child is accommodated or under a care order. The agency is required under the Children Act to take the initiative in developing care plans with families with children in placement. As part of this care plan, the agency must develop a plan that allows children to have contact with their parents, with siblings who may be placed elsewhere, and with other significant relatives and former carers. Decisions to restrict or terminate contact with any significant person must be fully justified. The care and contact plans should be reviewed at each statutory review.

Planning must involve parents, children, and others

The principle of client involvement in planning has been reinforced by the Children Act. Yet it is a principle that is often set aside, especially when clients are unresponsive or hostile. But if they are to be expected to comply with plans, parents must be involved in developing the plans. Moreover, when change depends not only on the parents, but also on the child, as is the case with older children, the child must also be involved. Children, especially adolescents, can easily subvert the best made plan. Their co-operation is essential.

Gathering and assessing the information needed to develop sound visiting plans requires collaboration with others. Visiting plans that best support the care plan reflect accurate, current information from service providers concerning the progress of parents. The person supervising visits has valuable information regarding parent-child interactions. Others, including substitute carers and children's teachers, may also have pertinent information. Case conferences or reviews are usually an efficient and effective way to pool and assess information for planning.

No one is free from biases. All of us welcome support when making difficult decisions. Therefore, planning visiting, as any other decision making, is strengthened by discussion with supervisors and peers. Case conferences and team decision-making generate creative options, decrease the influence of personal bias on case decisions, and reduce the stresses associated with planning visiting and services.

The plan must be known to all essential persons
All persons involved in visiting and in providing related services must be familiar with the plans. When everyone essential to the success of a plan is aware of it, individuals are less likely to be working at cross-purposes and the probability of achieving goals is increased.

It is therefore important that the original plan be in writing and that as the visiting plan is changed, any changes be specified in writing and a copy given to everyone who is involved in carrying out the plan. It is also important that parents know their rights and know what to do if they are not happy with a visiting plan.

There is a preferred contact plan
There is a preferred contact plan in every case that will best meet individual children's and parents' needs and will fit in with the care plan. You may respond to this statement by saying, 'But that's the ideal . . .' Yes, it is the ideal. Reaching for the ideal in a plan does not deny the

realities that may affect implementation; but assuming that the preferred or ideal plan can never be implemented guarantees that we will fall short of our standard. Determining the preferred plan encourages social workers, substitute carers, and other professionals to identify and try to eliminate obstacles to implementation. Moreover, developing a preferred plan can encourage practice that is less crisis oriented.

Developing contact plans is complicated

Developing sound contact plans, including visits and other forms of contact, is not easy. In fact, social workers who find visit planning easy or clear-cut are likely to be overlooking something. This complex process requires that changing yet current information be gathered continually from several sources. For example, you need to know the current schedules of the child, the parents, the carers, and persons transporting others to or supervising visits. Developing plans also requires knowledge about human development, behaviour, and change, and skill in making professional judgements, including the assessment of risk and of family progress.

The development of visiting plans is complicated by needing to establish contingency plans which anticipate and plan for the unpredictable. When people are under stress, their feelings are intense and their behaviours are often impulsive. Although human behaviour is never fully predictable, you must project the answers to questions such as these: 'Might the child be harmed or abducted during the visit?' and 'Will the parent arrive for the visit sober?'

Conflicts in determining the preferred plan are inevitable

The needs, requests, and expectations of those affected by the visiting plan often conflict, suggesting different perceptions of the preferred visiting plan. For example, a parent's right to frequent and increasingly unrestricted contact may conflict with the child's expressed preference. Parents' and foster carers' preferences concerning visit frequency or other arrangements may conflict. These conflicts are inevitable, but they must and can be resolved. The following considerations guide the resolution of such conflicts:

– Conflicts involving realistic concerns for a child's safety and security should be resolved by weighing this concern more heavily than any other.

– When the family members' right to contact conflicts with the needs or preferences of substitute carers or social workers, the conflict should be resolved in a way that protects and assures the family members' right to contact.

– When contact options offer varying degrees of support to the care plan, for example, with regard to frequency, length or venue of visits, weight should be given to the plan that best supports the care plan, even when that plan is less convenient or requires additional agency resources.

– When expectations as to who should be included in visits differ, the child's and the parents' preferences should, whenever possible, be given priority over those of substitute carers or extended family members.

– When limited resources create a conflict with any aspect of the preferred visiting plan, every effort should be made to develop or access resources in order to carry out the preferred plan.

The plan must reflect careful assessment of risk

The reason for compulsory removal of children from their own homes is to prevent harm.[1] Therefore, for children on care orders, most decisions concerning contact involve assessment of risk to the child. It must be emphasised that with regard to visit planning, risk assessment must be current and specific to the situation. Depending on the family's co-operation and current situation, risk to a child may increase or decrease within a brief period of time.

The parents' ability and willingness to care appropriately for, relate to, and protect the child affect all aspects of the visit arrangements. Continual assessment of parental behaviours and of abilities that relate to the reason for placement and the risk to the child is therefore essential. Several frameworks for risk assessment are available and are useful in risk assessment as it relates to visit planning.[2,3]

Since risk assessment is case-specific, you cannot automatically generalise from one family to another. The fact that one child was harmed in a particular visiting situation does not mean that all children on your case load in that situation are vulnerable.

A critical aspect of risk assessment is determining whether a child is being harmed during visits. Many children present behaviours following visits that are troublesome and distressing to substitute carers. It is not uncommon, for example, for children to be enuretic for several nights following a visit, to withdraw to their rooms immediately upon returning from a visit, to reject carers, to be argumentative, or to be less well behaved. Behaviours such as these are often interpreted by carers and social workers as indicators that the visits were harmful, leading almost always to efforts to decrease the frequency and length of visits or to hold visits at a venue other than the child's home.

But do these behaviours necessarily indicate that the children are being harmed? The answer in the vast majority of cases is no. Visiting disrupts a child's routine, can be physically tiring, and inevitably stirs deep feelings in a child, feelings that most children have difficulty verbalising. The troubled behaviour following visits is typically the result of fatigue and the disruption of routine and reflects the child's attachment to parents and the pain of separation.

There are times, however, when the behaviours just discussed and other behaviours do indicate that the children are being harmed. Indications of distress can be distinguished from harm only by observing the children and parents and by talking to the children. Does the child visibly cringe at a parent's touch? Does the child continue to cling to you well into the visit rather that go to a parent? Is there physical evidence of abuse? Do the behaviours described above persist for days after the visit and interfere with the child's functioning in many areas? What does the child say when asked to describe the visit?

If it appears that the child is reacting to the pain of separation, you might consider increasing the frequency of visits. Frequent visits more easily become a part of a child's routine and are therefore less disruptive. More frequent visits can ease the pain of each goodbye. If there is evidence of harm during unsupervised visits, however, the plan must be changed to allow only closely supervised visits, and an evaluation must be completed regarding the impact of visiting on the child.

Visit arrangements should never be used as rewards or punishments
Visit arrangements directly depend on assessment of the parents' ability

and of the risk to the child. As parents can assume greater responsibility for child care and supervision, visits are planned more often, for longer periods, more frequently in the parents' home, and with fewer restrictions. Arrangements, therefore, are a logical consequence of the assessment of parenting behaviours and the family situation. They are not a reward.

The distinction between perceiving changes in visiting arrangements as a logical consequence or as a reward is quite important. When you view changes in visiting as directly related to assessment of changes in families, visiting arrangements can be developed openly and as part of the agency's care plan. When social workers or other service providers (for example, treatment facilities) use visits to reward behaviours of parents or children, such as keeping appointments, they misuse the authority inherent in their position. Further, family members may assume that co-operation with a plan, rather than change in behaviour, is all they need to demonstrate. Equating progress solely with service use leads to false assumptions of change by social workers that may ultimately endanger the child and undermine achievement of case objectives.

When parents do not make the personal or situational changes required to assure the safety of children, maintaining a more restrictive visiting plan is not a punishment, it is a means of child protection. Rather than promising increased visiting as a leverage or an incentive, you should deal directly with the lack of progress. Are services inappropriate or ineffective? Are there obstacles to service use? Are the parents ambivalent about contact with their child or about family reunification?

When visit arrangements are viewed by the social worker and the family as either rewards or punishments for either parents or children, the social worker's authority over plan changes is magnified. Family members' fears of the misuse of this authority, ever present, are likely to be heightened and become an obstacle in the client–social worker relationship. Visit changes may then easily be perceived as (and may be) capricious or punitive. You can help parents and children understand that visits are not used as rewards or punishments by acknowledging in your initial discussion with them that many families fear that visiting may be used in this way. Describe the relationship between visiting arrangements and the assessment of change in families. Then, throughout the placement, openly discuss the reasons for all visiting decisions.

Children and parents have a right to see each other. That right should be restricted only when there is a danger to the child. As the danger decreases or increases, so does the restriction. It has nothing to do with reward and punishment.

Elements of the visiting plan

The visiting plan should reflect the purpose of contact and should specify the following elements:

- frequency, venue and length of scheduled visits
- if and how visits are to be supervised
- who is to participate in the visits
- tasks that are to be accomplished during visits
- agency and parental responsibilities related to visits

Each of these elements is discussed below. As you read, you should keep in mind that none of these elements remains static during the course of a child's placement. Instead, as we will discuss later, predictable changes should occur as the time for reunification nears or as the agency works to achieve an alternative permanent placement. In addition, changes that cannot be predicted may be necessary when crises occur, such as hospitalisation or death in the child's or carer's families.

Frequency

Visit frequency includes both how quickly after placement the first contact visit occurs and how often visiting occurs throughout the placement. We believe that the first visit should occur within 48 hours of the placement to reassure children that their parents have not abandoned them. Weekly visits should be viewed as essential. A minimum frequency of weekly visits is particularly important for young children whose memory span is very short. Older children, who are to return home, will usually benefit from seeing their family at least once a week. As the time for reunification nears, visits should occur more often than once a week.

Length

Visit length may range from an hour to several days. As discussed later, visit length must provide sufficient time for natural interaction and for completion of activities related to the care plan.

Venue

The choice of venue for visits should be only as restrictive as is necessary to assure the child's safety, allow for privacy and for natural interaction, and whenever possible be in the parents' home. The venue should reflect the purpose of the visit and be identified in the visit plan.

Supervision

Visits in some cases may need to be supervised in order to protect children, assess and record interaction, or teach parents. Visits may be supervised by different persons at different times depending on the purpose of the supervision. The purpose of supervision and the identity of the persons supervising (i.e. social worker, foster carer, family aide, visiting nurse, or volunteer) should be included in the contact plan.

Participants

The contact plan should specify who may or may not visit and by what process the agency will consider exceptions. Most children in placement have a significant relationship with persons other than their parents – grandparents, friends of their parents, previous substitute carers, or others. When this is the case, these persons should be included in at least some visits if the child requests it and if their presence does not endanger the child or subvert achievement of goals.

Supportive services

Services to facilitate visiting are often necessary and should be spelt out in the visiting plan. Who will transport the child? Are the parents responsible for their transport? Will any financial assistance be provided to the parents? Will the agency provide child care for children who are living at home?

Activities

Parents may be encouraged to perform specific tasks related to child care during visits. These activities should be appropriate to the developmental age of the child and facilitate natural interaction between parent and child. Examples of appropriate visiting activities include accompanying the child to medical and dental appointments, shopping for clothes, and attending school conferences and open days. When parents are expected to perform certain tasks, this should be clearly stated in the plan.

Conditions

In individual cases, parents may be required to meet conditions related to visits. For example, a parent may be required to phone in advance to confirm his/her intention to keep a visit appointment, to remain sober throughout the visit, to refrain from promising at each visit to take the child home at the end of the visit, to refrain from using physical discipline, or to refrain from bringing other persons to the visit without prior approval. Any such conditions must be specified in the care plan.

Placement phases

Work with most children in placement follows a rather predictable sequence. Immediately before and following placement, the emphasis is on assessment, goal setting, and care planning. Following this initial phase, which should be completed as quickly yet as thoroughly as possible, the agency and family work together to make the changes necessary for the child to return home. We have termed this phase the central phase. Activity during this phase will determine the outcome of the plan. This phase will often extend over several months or occasionally years. Reunification is the final placement phase in the majority of cases, beginning when the planning group of parents, carers and social worker makes specific plans for return. This phase of placement ends when parents assume full-time care and custody, with the agency's, and if necessary, the court's approval. The emphasis in this phase is on facilitating a smooth transition from placement to home and determining what services will be provided after the child has returned home. In cases when the child cannot return home, the central phase is followed by a new planning phase during which long-term goals are established.

Visiting phases

Predictable changes in the visiting plan correspond to each placement phase. These changes concern both visit purposes and arrangements.

Changing purposes of visiting

As discussed in Chapter 1, visiting has many purposes. Visiting can provide an opportunity for workers to:
— assess the parent–child relationship
— assess the parents' ability to care for and relate to the child adequately and appropriately
— help the parents develop appropriate parenting behaviours
— help the child interact with the parents
— identify and resolve problems before the child returns home
— evaluate the family's progress towards targeted changes
— assess the feasibility and timing of the child's return home
— facilitate the child's transition to the parents' home

Although each purpose may apply to some extent throughout all the phases of placement, each is not of equal importance during each phase. For example, visiting may be used primarily for assessment during the initial phase. While assessment continues throughout placement, visiting is used less for assessment and more for teaching and for problem identification and resolution during the central phase. Visiting is used during the reunification phase primarily to ease the transition from placement to home and to determine what services will be needed to support the family following reunification. As you use visiting for specific objectives, however, you should keep in mind that when the goal is reunification, the underlying and most important purpose of visiting through all phases of placement is always to maintain parent–child attachment.

Changing visit arrangements

You should develop the initial visiting plan with the expectation that changes will have to be made often, but only as part of a flexible plan. When the goal is return home and the family progresses towards that goal, visit arrangement changes should follow a planned and predictable sequence. Over time, visits will be more frequent and occur more often in the child's own home. They will be longer and less supervised. In short, as reunification nears, the primary responsibility for the child's care and protection during visits shifts from the agency to the parents.

Visiting plans during the initial assessment phase

Many children are looked after in local authority care as a result of professional judgements that, even with the use of family support services, their needs cannot be met if they remain at home. Occasionally placement occurs because a parent is hospitalised or imprisoned. Regardless of the reason for placement, the extent to which the agency controls visiting arrangements and supervises visits throughout the placement should depend on the parents' ability at any point in time to care for the child appropriately and the child's level of security with the parents.

Immediately following placement, the child and parents are often uncomfortable with each other. This is a typical reaction to placement. In their frustration and anger about the child's placement, parents may blame the child for the placement. Sometimes parents pressurise their children to recant their allegations of maltreatment. If the child had to be placed before family support services could be provided, there may be little information available about the family. If placement is the result of a parent's or child's treatment needs or a parent's imprisonment, confusion may exist about the duration and probable outcome of the placement. Regardless of the circumstances, placement is usually a devastating event for both parents and children, and visiting initially is awkward.

During the first month following placement, you will therefore typically need to supervise visits and to carefully control the venue of visits, their length, and participants. By doing so you can ease the awkwardness of visits by facilitating interaction between parents and children. You can protect the child as needed. You can gather important information about the parent–child relationship and patterns of interaction. But whatever the reason for your presence during visits, you should remember that the primary purpose of visiting is to maintain the relationship between parent and child. Unless the child would be endangered, allow some time for the parent and child to be alone.

The initial visits, even when closely supervised, should be conducted in the most natural setting possible – the child's home, the foster home, or a comfortable visiting room. Natural interaction is simply impossible in a room with a desk and four chairs, and observation under such circumstances will be of limited use.

Visiting plans during the central phase
As the family's needs are identified and the family begins to make the changes necessary for the child's return home, the work enters the central phase. Visit arrangements continue to reflect the agency's responsibility to assure the child's safety and security, but they will also be used to achieve care goals. Visits provide a crucial opportunity for parents and children to learn and practise new skills and patterns of behaviour together. Visits also allow for further identification and resolution of family problems. From the perspective of both the agency and the family, visiting during the central phase provides experiences and information necessary for assessing the feasibility and timing of the child's return home.

One could think of visits during the central phase as an "apprenticeship" in family functioning. Family members try to apply what they have learned. As they succeed within a particular visiting arrangement, changes in the arrangement should be made to allow for further progression towards the child's return home. When families do not succeed, you have to assess whether changes in the visiting arrangements or in service provision could provide greater support for success. For example, perhaps the parents need someone present during visits to give immediate suggestions and feedback regarding their care of the children.

The visit plan during the central phase should specify that visits will incrementally occur more often and be longer. To illustrate, a young mother whose baby was placed for failure to thrive visited in the foster home three mornings a week for two hours each morning, helping with feeding and bathing. For three weeks the mother kept to the visiting programme, worked at caring for her child, and responded better to the child's needs. The visit plan was then changed to visits for the entire morning on two of the three days a week with less involvement of the foster mother, allowing the birth mother greater responsibility for the child's care for a longer period, including two feedings. After three weeks with longer visits, an additional morning-long visit was to be scheduled weekly, but in the mother's own home with supervision provided by a family aide. These incremental steps reflected the agency's expectation that the mother assume more responsibility for her child's care as quickly as she was able, but improved the likelihood of success with each step by assuring that her child would be adequately cared for and safe during the process.

As illustrated in this example, agency supervision should diminish as responsibility is gradually shifted to the parents. In a visit in an office or family centre, for instance, the supervisor might initially participate in the visit and intervene when indicated, then change to sitting in the room listening, but focusing on paperwork, then later occasionally observe through a one-way mirror, and finally be available in another room should the parents or child request assistance. Eventually, the visits might take place in public, away from the office or family centre, in the child's foster home, or in the child's own home, again with decreasing degrees of monitoring. At a certain point, non-family members, such as the parents' and child's friends, may be included in the visits. Increased flexibility concerning both visit location and participants allows for more natural interaction. The family and child are thus supported in moving towards reunification.

Orchestrating a family's successful progression through the sequence of changes in arrangements requires making informed judgments about the child's safety, constant integrating of the visit plan with other aspects of the family's care plan, and time. Time must be invested in preparing the child, the child's parents, and the substitute carers for the visit, and in co-ordinating and careful monitoring of visit arrangements. Guidelines for assisting families through this sequence are provided in the following chapters.

Two changes that occur during the central phase are critical with regard to the shift from agency to parental responsibility: the point at which visits are no longer supervised, and the point at which the child stays overnight in the parents' home. Both require particular attention to risk assessment, and to support for the parents, child, and the child's substitute carers – topics that will be discussed in chapters that follow. Approval of these changes should be given by senior management or courts if appropriate.

Parents whose children are accommodated retain their parental rights. When children are the subject of care orders, the importance of the shift from agency to parental responsibility cannot be overstated. A judgement that a child is ready to return home is premature until the family has had the opportunity to carry full child care responsibilities unsupervised and overnight, and until social workers and the family determine that the child is safe in those situations. (See The Placement of Children with Parents etc. Regulations, 1991.)

Visiting during the reunification phase
The reunification phase of the placement is marked by a shift in care planning. Rather than assessing the feasibility of returning home, emphasis is placed on assuring a smooth transition from placement to family home, on determining when parents can assume full-time care, and on identifying services to support the family following reunification. Successful reunification may be doomed if it occurs precipitously, and if the family does not have opportunities to identify and resolve problems before the child returns home. The family must be able to experience gradually the changes that occur in the family system as the child is home for longer visits and parents assume greater responsibility for the child's care.

The use of visiting to facilitate successful reunification is illustrated in the following case. Reunification was planned for two children in January. During September, the children had visits at home that began after school on Friday and ended late Saturday afternoon, according to plan. In mid-October, the half-term holiday provided the opportunity for a four-day visit. The Friday afternoon through to Saturday afternoon visits then continued until the end of November, when the plan called for the children to live at home during the week and at the foster home at weekends. This arrangement enabled the parents to readjust to the responsibility for daily care and to getting the children to school while providing for respite during the transition. This continued for four weeks upto mid-December, when the children's school holiday began. At this point, the plan provided for an extended visit at home, with the assumption that if the transition continued to go well, the children would then remain full-time in their parents' care. In early January, the agency and family members agreed that return home was a viable plan.

Clearly, a visiting plan of this nature requires the commitment of the agency and the substitute carers to a transition period that eases the major changes families must cope with at reunification. Visits during this period must provide maximum opportunity for parent–child contact, for parental responsibility for the child, particularly in areas where breakdown previously occurred, and for evaluation of remaining stress points. These arrangements are successful if they, on the one hand, facilitate the child's successful move home, or, on the other hand, forestall premature reunification by identifying important unresolved problems.

In many cases where more than one child in a family is in placement, not all children will return home at the same time. Visit planning must be carefully individualised with particular attention to the needs of each child.

Visiting plans when reunification is not the goal

Visiting does not end when it is determined that reunification is not the goal. First, it must be remembered that unless contact is terminated by court order, parents and children have the right to contact, which may include visits. An agency decision against reunification in and of itself does not abrogate this right. Second, visiting continues to play a vital role in the care plan, a role that in some cases is time-limited and that in others will continue indefinitely.

Through visiting, you can assist the family members, particularly the child, in dealing with the planned change in their relationship whether or not there is a plan for continuing contact in the future. In most instances, the change in care goal reflects the parents' unwillingness or inability to make the changes necessary for the child to return home. Children must be helped to understand why they cannot return home, the nature of the relationship they will have with their parents in the future, and the alternative permanency plan. They must be helped to work through their feelings about this reality, and visiting is an important part of this process.

When the goal is independent living or long-term placement, and both the child and the parents are interested in maintaining contact, the plans should provide for continuing contact unless there is compelling justification to the contrary. Continuing contact can help the child develop self-esteem and a positive identity, and it can maintain family relationships that may endure and support the child when agency service ends.[4]

In instances where all contact will be disconnected, you should consider planning a visit and/or other contacts, such as letters for goodbyes, and rituals related to goodbyes, such as picture taking. Often, because of your own discomfort or concern to protect a child, you may interpret children's seeming lack of interest in seeing their parents as an indication that they have forgotten them or do not want contact. This interpretation is usually incorrect. In fact, many children in placement need permission to show and talk about their feelings. Planning a goodbye visit gives this permission. The visits themselves can help family members accept the reality of changed or ending relationships, contributing vitally to the grieving and healing process for both children and parents.

Individual considerations

This chapter has discussed the assumptions that underpin planning, the phases through which children in placement typically pass, and the visiting plans that correspond to these phases of placement. This discussion might have seemed to suggest that all you need to know to develop the visiting plan is the care goal and the phase of placement. As you know from experience, this is far from true. Visiting plans depend not only on the care goal and phase of placement but also on a variety of factors unique to each situation that relate primarily to each child's characteristics and needs, to each parent's functioning, and to family relationships. Visiting plans for children are also affected by their substitute carer's capacity and willingness to be involved in various aspects of visiting.

Throughout a placement, specific information concerning the child, the child's parents, and the child's substitute carers shapes the visiting plan. None of the information gathered stands alone. For example, both the child's needs and parents' functioning must not only be assessed, but also examined in terms of the current fit between them. Ways in which specific information regarding the child, the parents, family relationships, and the substitute carers shape the plan are identified in the next three chapters.

References

1 Adcock M, White R, Hollows A, *Significant Harm: Its management outcome*, Significant Publications, 1991

2 Magura S, Moses B S, and Jones M A, *Assessing Risk and Measuring Change in Families: The family risk scales*, Child Welfare League of America, 1987, USA

3 Snyder E, and Ramo K, *Deciding To Place or Not To Place*, School of Social Work and Human Services, Eastern Washington University, 1983, USA

4 Wedge P and Mantle G, *Sibling Groups and Social Work*, Avebury Gower, 1991

3 Specific considerations: the child

The preferred visiting plan depends in part on the child's age, requests regarding visits, reactions to visits, developmental and therapeutic needs, and schedule.

Children's chronological and developmental age

Each child's actual age and developmental age may differ. Many children in foster care and residential group placements do not function at the developmental levels their ages would suggest. Because of the unique abilities and needs of each child, it is not possible to provide hard-and-fast age-related guidelines for visiting. Some generalisations, however, are possible. For example, no matter what the developmental age, infants and toddlers are unable to provide self-care and supervision, and they cannot sustain the memory of their parents without very frequent contact. Therefore, the child's actual and developmental ages suggest answers to the following questions that must be raised in each case in planning visits.

How frequently does this child need to have contact with parents to preserve and build the parent–child relationship?
Understanding the child's age-related sense of time helps you anticipate how the child will experience the absence of parents between each visit and to plan frequency of visiting accordingly. The child's sense of time has been described by well-known theorists as 'the interval before a leave-taking will be experienced as a permanent loss, accompanied by feelings of helplessness and profound deprivation.'[1] From an adult perspective, one week without parent–child contact goes quickly. For the baby or toddler, seven days are an eternity. Children's experiences of separation are shaped by their ability to retain the memory or image of their absent parents. As memory develops with age, children can recall that their parents returned following previous separations. This capacity

increases children's ability to understand and tolerate their parents' leaving and returning.

The child's age and sense of time, therefore, are primary considerations in planning frequency of visits. As noted earlier, visits should occur at least weekly. For babies, toddlers, and preschool children, contact more often than weekly is warranted from the beginning of placement to decrease the child's sense of abandonment, to protect the parent–child attachment, and to assist the child in moving from one home to another.

What is the child's capacity for self-care?

In planning visit length, supervision, and location, you must consider the child's capacity for self-care. Capacity is related in large part to developmental age, but it also relates to the special needs of the child. The degree of this capacity depends on the reason for placement and the parents' functioning at any point in time. To illustrate, school-age children who can follow instructions, make sandwiches, and dress without help will be at less risk during lengthy unsupervised visits at home with a parent who has been neglectful than a baby or toddler will be. Similarly, an eight-year-old whose development has progressed age-appropriately will be at less risk than an eight-year-old who is developmentally delayed or whose special needs complicate self-care.

How vulnerable is this child should potentially harmful situations occur during a visit?

Actual and developmental ages similarly affect a child's ability to recognise a potentially volatile or dangerous situation, leave the situation, and/or call for help, all of which influence the choices for supervision, duration, and location of visits. Because some children may not be willing to ask for help during a visit when doing so means exposing their parents' problematic behaviours, the assessment of the child's vulnerability must address this factor as well as the child's age and capacity.

The ability of children to protect themselves is particularly important during the central and reunification phases as families show progress and unsupervised home visits are being considered. For example, children of parents who have demonstrated progress in their recovery from substance abuse, in managing anger, or in complying with treatment for mental illness may differ in their ability to recognise and cope with potentially harmful situations. If a parent who is a recovering alcoholic begins to drink during an unsupervised visit, a child even as young as six or seven may be able to call a neighbour, the worker, substitute carer, or police for help in getting away from the situation. Younger or less capable children visiting with the same parent during the same placement phase will need more protection during visits, and unsupervised home visits may be delayed until the parent demonstrates more appropriate behaviour.

How able is this child to structure his or her own activities during a visit? Children's temperaments, as well as their ages, influence what they can manage or tolerate during visits. Does a child become bored and irritable easily? Is a child unable to entertain him or herself for a period of time while their mother cares for younger siblings? If so, it might be useful to have someone present during visits – particularly those that occur early in the placement – to help parents attend to the child. In addition, it is useful to identify activities that the child and parent enjoyed before placement and plan visits to include them. Walks, trips to park playgrounds, playing games, and playing with dolls or other toys are all appropriate activities that can extend the interaction between younger children and parents. Older children may need to see friends as well as family when visiting home.

Children's wishes

Children indicate preferences about visit arrangements both directly –'Please stay with me while I'm with my dad,' – and indirectly – 'You haven't sat in on my visits with dad for a while.' However expressed, you should try to determine what is behind a child's request before making or changing visiting arrangements. The following example illustrates the importance of understanding what the child's concerns or interests are.

Sara, an eight-year-old, asked her social worker if it would be all right for her to see her family less often. When her worker explored what prompted this request, it was clear that Sara actually looked forward to her visits and enjoyed being with both of her parents. Further exploration revealed that Sara had overheard her foster carers discussing their unhappiness with the frequency of visits. She was afraid that they were angry with her for wanting to see her parents and worried that they were going to ask that she be moved.

In this instance, intervention with the foster carers, not a change in visit frequency, was indicated. In contrast, in exploring a similar request you might find that a child prefers less frequent visits because he or she is frightened. A decrease in visit frequency, however, may still be inappropriate. Fears might better be allayed by helping the parents understand how their behaviour threatens the child, by more closely supervising the visits, or by changing the location of the visits.

As you prepare children for visits and observe their reactions after visits, you must not only identify but also try to understand their requests and reactions. Your understanding then helps you decide what response is appropriate.

Children's reactions to visits

Visits seem to present a Catch 22 for children. When children are not visited, they feel abandoned and become estranged from their families. But when children are visited, they often experience distress in anticipation of the visit, during the visit, in separating from their parents as the visit ends, and during the separation immediately following the visit. Those providing children's daily care – foster carers and child care workers – are often asked to record and report children's reactions. When the reactions present their carers with management problems, such as disobedience, they may demand less frequent or shorter visits. You may also directly observe a child's distress and automatically conclude that less contact with the parent would be helpful. Before determining whether, or in what ways, the plan should be altered, however, each of the following four questions should be answered.

Is the child's reaction normal given the stresses of placement?
As discussed earlier, many children experience distress related to the end of each visit and to the separation following visits. An increase in frequency and/or duration of visits may relieve this distress and should be considered. More frequent and longer visits increase the ability of most children to cope with the separation and to adjust to placement. In

addition, telephone calls and letters between visits can ease the pain of separation.

Does the child's reaction reflect distress related to conflicting loyalties?
Placement inevitably places children in a double bind. They are expected to fit in with foster carers or a residential group, while simultaneously maintaining their identification with their family. When substitute carers support visits and accept children's affection for and identification with their families, children are freer to talk about and examine their intense, often ambivalent, feelings about family, visiting, and return home.

Children who are either subtly or openly encouraged to shift their loyalty and their primary affections to the substitute carers are in a no-win position. They feel guilty and confused. They may act as if they prefer not to be with their parents to avoid displeasing the substitute carers with whom, after all, they spend most of their time. They are likely to repress their reactions, and the result may be problematic behaviour, withdrawal, or depression.

Children are also sometimes confronted by their parents' demand that they do not co-operate with their foster carers or child care workers: 'They're not your parents, you don't have to obey them.' This, too, places children in a no-win position.

When children's reactions to visits reflect even in part the lack of their substitute carers' support for their relationship with their families, immediate intervention is necessary. Intervention typically involves counselling with children and substitute carers to help them deal with the difficult situation the placement has created. If substitute carers are unable to support visiting, even after your interventions, a move may be necessary. Also, where parents undermine the child's efforts to adjust to the placement, intervention with the child and the parents is indicated.

Does the child's reaction reveal problems in the visiting situation?
When children are distressed by the visiting situation, changes in the visit arrangements and/or other interventions may be indicated. In many instances, families need continual assistance in planning and structuring visits. Parents often need your repeated help in thinking through what activities are age-appropriate, of interest to the child, and suited to the

length and location of the visit. Parents sometimes need help in planning reasonably healthy snacks or meals. Repeated open discussion of appropriate visit rules and discipline helps decrease the discomfort for the child created by inconsistency between family and placement expectations.

Does the child's reaction indicate problems in the parent–child relationship?

When problems in the parent–child relationship contribute to the child's reaction to visits, additional diagnostic and therapeutic work is most likely indicated for the parents, child, and/or parents and child together. Problems of this nature are typically indicated by the intensity and persistence of the child's reaction as in the example below.

Gary, age ten, who had been physically abused by his father, had weekly supervised visits with him in an agency visiting room. Not only was the child's extreme discomfort with his father obvious during the visits, but Gary also developed a pattern of problematic behaviours in school on visiting days only. He had been warned by his teacher that when he misbehaved, he would have to stay after school. Thus, his misbehaviour was resulting in his being late for, or missing, visits.

When relationship problems appear to be harmful to the children, the agency should document the behaviours of the parents and the reactions of the children and, if necessary, apply to court for variation of a contact order. The burden of demonstrating the association between the parents' behaviours, the children's reactions, and harm to the children falls on the social worker. Therefore, consistent specific documentation of directly observed interactions is necessary. Whenever visits are considered harmful, agency supervision for the purposes of child protection, assessment, and documentation is essential.

Children's developmental tasks

The children you work with may be thought of as children in placement rather than as children. Their developmental tasks (which may or may not coincide with their actual age) may be overlooked as intervention focuses on improvement of their parents' functioning. In reality, children who are in placement, like all children, are growing physically,

Figure 1

Developmentally related visit activities

Age	Developmental tasks	Developmentally related visit activities
Infancy (0-2)	Develop primary attachment	Meet basic needs (feeding, changing, holding, cuddling)
	Develop object permanence	Play peek-a-boo games
	Basic motor development (sit, reach, stand, crawl, walk)	Help with standing, walking, etc., by holding hand, play "come to me" games
	Word recognition	Name objects, repeat name games, read picture books
	Begin exploration and mastery of the environment	Encourage exploration: take walks; play together with colourful, noisy, moving items
Toddler (2-4)	Develop impulse control	Make and consistently enforce rules
	Language development	Read simple stories; play games
	Imitation, fantasy play	Play "let's pretend" games; encourage imitative play by doing things together such as "clean house", "go to the shops"
		Play together at park; assist in learning to ride tricycle; dance together to music
	Small motor co-ordination	Draw together; string beads together
	Develop basic sense of time	Discuss visits and visit activities in terms of "after breakfast", "after lunch", "before supper", etc.
	Identify and assert preferences	Allow choices in activities, clothes worn, foods eaten

Stage	Developmental task	Suggested activities
Preschool/ early school (5-7)	Gender identification	Be open to discussing boy–girl physical differences
		Be open to discussing child's perception of gender roles; read books together
	Continuing development of conscience	Make and enforce consistent rules; discuss consequences of behaviour
	Develop ability to solve problems	Encourage choices in activities
	Learning cause–effect relationships	Point out cause–effect and logical consequences of actions
	Task completion and order	Plan activities with beginning, middle, end (as prepare, make cake, clean up)
		Play simple games
	School entry and adjustment	Shop for school clothes together; provide birth certificate, medical record required for school entry; go with child to visit school, playground prior to first day; accompany child to school
School-age (8-12)	Skill development (school, sports, special interests)	Help with homework; practise sports together; demonstrate support of special interests, such as help with collections; attend school conferences and activities; work together on household tasks
	Peer group development and team play	Involve peers in visit activities
		Attend sports activities with child (child's team or observe sports together)
	Development of self-awareness	Be open to talking with child
	Preparation for puberty	Discuss physical changes expected; answer questions openly

emotionally, socially, and intellectually and need the help of their parents, as well as their substitute carers, to accomplish developmental tasks.

The child's current developmental tasks should be considered in planning visits. Some suggested activities for younger children are presented in Figure 1. Well-equipped visiting rooms and opportunities to talk about the parents' role in activities support parents in following through many of these activities. Activities for older children and adolescents should reinforce their schoolwork and other interests. Certain parental behaviours support adolescents' development, such as setting firm but flexible limits, commenting positively about a young person's changing appearance, and supporting the young person in making decisions about his or her future.

Attention to the children's current developmental tasks in planning visits encourages parents to have reasonable expectations of their children. It also allows parents to assess their ability to parent, and it helps children to trust and gain confidence in their parents. All these factors are essential to successful reunification.

Children's therapeutic needs

Children's experiences in life or their special needs may also often determine visiting arrangements. For example, a girl who has been molested by her mother's boyfriend may at a point in her own treatment need to directly challenge her mother's denial of knowledge of the abuse. Visit planning during this period of her treatment should support her therapeutic tasks and anticipate her need for visit supervision, privacy, and flexibility in timing.

Physical therapy or medical treatment may limit children's mobility and thus the visit location. For example, some children are scheduled routinely for inpatient medical care or observation. Who will be allowed to visit during hospitalisations? If hospital visiting must be supervised, who will be responsible for arranging it? In addition, involving parents in the children's care during visits in the hospital, in the foster home, or in the parents' home may require that the parents be trained by health care staff and that visits be supervised until the parents' ability to follow procedures appropriately can be assessed.

The therapeutic needs of children may also be prompted in part by the care goal as in the following example.

Julie, age seven, and her nine-year-old sister, Janice, had been in foster care for three years and return home was not a feasible plan for them. They were subjects of care orders. They continued to have supervised visits with their mother, but they were eager for their foster carers to adopt them, as the agency planned, and for contact with their mother to end. She was unpredictable and sometimes quite harsh. When the court ruled that the parents' contact be terminated, however, the children requested a final meeting with their mother. Janice said they had things they wanted to tell her and they wanted photographs of the three of them together. The worker was very concerned about the mother's behaviour towards the girls and about the direction the visit might take. It was clear, though, that the visit could have a therapeutic purpose in moving the girls into a permanent relationship with their adopting foster carers. With the assistance of the girls, the mother, and the foster carers, the worker planned a brief visit in an agency visiting room that was to focus upon photograph taking. The visit included the foster carers, with whom the mother had had frequent contact, and the mother's best friend. The children made an audiotape for their mother with their messages to her and gave this to her at the visit, asking that she play it later. Thus, the children's need to express their feelings and to have a goodbye ritual of taking photographs was met. Potentially hurtful dialogue was avoided by carefully structuring the visit location, length, and participants, and by closely supervising the visit.

Children's schedules

Children's schedules include their ordinary daily routines of mealtimes, rest-times, playtimes, bathing, and bedtimes, as well as regular activities, such as school, treatment appointments, and after school clubs or classes. Whenever possible, visits should be arranged to involve parents in the children's routines, particularly when the children cannot return home until the parents are better able to provide ordinary daily care. Imagine a parent visiting her eighteen-month-old son from 10 am to 11.30 am, after he has had breakfast and played and is ready for a sleep. She is likely to be frustrated either because he sleeps through the visit or because he is thrown off his schedule and is miserable. It is better to arrange her visit earlier or later so that she can participate in a typical feeding and wakeful period.

You must anticipate and try to avoid creating problems in the child's usual routine by the way in which visits are scheduled. For example, foster carers often complain that children's appetites are spoiled by snacks provided by parents during after-school visits. In many instances, however, deliberately scheduling visits to include a snack or meal to provide an appropriate, routine focus for a part of the visit gives parents an opportunity to meet this basic need adequately, and clarifies for carers that the children will not need to be fed immediately upon returning to the placement.

Beginning and ending visits at transition points already in children's schedules may ease the separation for them. For example, visits can begin immediately after school rather than later in the afternoon, or end when children go to school on Monday morning rather than on Sunday evening.

Regular social activities should also be considered in planning visits. Older children, particularly, may resent missing an activity with their peers in order to see their relatives. Not only should children not be denied participation in activities such as ball games or school activities that are important to them, but whenever possible their parents should be invited to participate in the activities with them. You should be careful, however, that the schedules of children do not become too full for contact visits. While school activities and swimming, ballet, and piano lessons are important, placements where children's schedules have little room for visiting have to be looked into closely.

References

1 Goldstein J, Freud A, and Solnit A, *Beyond the Best Interests of the Child*, The Free Press, 1973, USA.

4 Specific considerations: parents and family relationships

Plans for contact should also take into account any parental behaviour that relates to the reason for placement and which must change for the child to return home; that relates to the nature of the parents' co-operation in carrying out the visiting plan; and that has endangered the child in visits during previous placements. Moreover, parents' wishes and requests regarding visiting arrangements, their reactions to visiting, and their own schedules are also factors to consider when planning contact.

In some cases, the visiting plan will be the same for both parents. In many cases, the plan will be different. The difference may reflect the fact that one parent was not a custodial parent before placement or it may reflect a difference in the parent's interest in or treatment of the child. It is important that you consider each parent individually as well as consider the family relationships and interactions.

Parental behaviour and abilities related to placement

The majority of children are placed due to parental actions or omissions that put them at grave risk, with reunification dependent on change in the parents' functioning. Contact planning should pay specific attention to the situations that will promote and support that change. Visit arrangements, therefore, should vary somewhat depending upon the parents' behaviours that relate to the reason for placement.

Whatever the reason for placement, the parents' knowledge of the child's needs and the appropriateness of the parents' expectations of the child must be considered in planning visits. When parents' understanding of their children's needs is inadequate, including someone else in visits who can both model appropriate responses to the child and instruct the parents assures that parents are given ample opportunity to learn about the specific needs of their child.

Neglect

Placement may result from the parents' neglect of the child's physical, emotional, or social needs; education; supervision; or medical care. Problems may exist with regard to housing and living conditions.

Visiting plans may vary in relation to the nature of and reasons for the parents' neglect. For example, if the parents are committed to, but unprepared for, parenthood, a comprehensive programme of education, development of social supports, and provision of additional resources may be indicated. Parents may participate in parenting courses or receive individualised instruction. In such instances, visits should allow the parents to care for the child in their own home with a family aide or other professional who instructs, provides feedback, models behaviours, and monitors the child's care. Visits must allow sufficient time for the parents to provide care in a realistic way. As the parents' abilities increase, so should the frequency and the length of visits.

If the parents' neglect reflects ambivalence about parenting in general or about parenting a particular child, the service will focus on helping parents to resolve their ambivalence and either commit themselves to parenting or work with the agency towards an adoptive placement or a placement with a relative. Visiting is also an essential component of this treatment process. Frequent, lengthy periods of time with the child help the parents confront their real feelings for the child, their willingness to be responsible for meeting the child's daily needs, and their ability to do so. With this group of parents, you must resist the temptation to succumb to a routine, weekly, hour-long visit. Ambivalent parents rarely ask for more, but routinised visiting prolongs indecision by providing an easy way out for ambivalent parents – continued contact without responsibility.

If the neglect results from housing problems or problems primarily with living conditions related to poverty, every effort should be made to find a place quickly where children and parents can visit in an atmosphere which encourages natural interaction. Neither extensive treatment nor supervision are indicated in such cases, and the primary, if not the only, function of visiting is to maintain the relationship between parents and children.

In cases where the parents reject children or are unwilling to assume parental responsibility, reunification may only briefly be the care goal, if at all. In such instances, contact should be closely supervised. If the visits are seen to be harmful to the child, action should be taken to limit or terminate the contact.

Physical abuse by parents

Abusive behaviour of parents may reflect inability to manage their own anger and impulses, limited awareness of effective child management techniques, or religious or philosophical commitment to corporal punishment. The nature, frequency, severity, and recency of the parents' abusing behaviour affect planning, particularly with regard to visit supervision and location. Planning is also affected by the parents' degree of acceptance of responsibility for their behaviour, and the progress made through rehabilitative efforts. As discussed previously, the child's age and capacity for self-protection are also critical considerations.

The planning of visiting for physically abusive parents requires the thoughtful input of all involved in the parents' treatment, as each change to increase the amount of contact and decrease the degree of supervision involves taking a carefully calculated risk. The responsibility for decisions to return children home will rest with a senior manager and such decisions are usually taken by child protection review conferences.

Sexual abuse by parents

Social workers report that particularly in sex abuse cases, parents may pressure their child to recant allegations, and the abuser may continue to abuse the child. During the initial assessment period, therefore, close supervision is required to determine whether the parents accept or challenge the child's allegations and to determine whether inappropriate touching is likely to recur. Until it has been determined that each parent consistently behaves appropriately with the child, whoever is supervising the visit should not leave the child alone with a parent.

In some cases of sexual abuse the child is removed from the home. In others, the courts may make prohibited steps orders to keep the abusing parent away from the child and home. Even when the parent is kept out of the home, the social worker has the responsibility to develop a visiting plan that is consistent with any contact order made by the court.

A parent's failure to protect a child

A common reason for placement is abuse not by a parent, but by someone who is living with the family or who is a frequent visitor in the home. Such persons might include step-parents, friends, relatives, and babysitters. Placement results not because a parent has been abusive or even neglectful in terms of providing routine care and supervision, but because the parent is unable or has failed to protect the child. Reunification in such cases is contingent largely on the progress of the parent and the abuser in treatment or on the parent's ability to separate from the abuser. Similarly, home visits without supervision are dependent on the parent's ability to protect the child. Visiting must be supervised until it is clear that the parent can do so. In such cases, visiting in the foster home or in the homes of relatives can offer safety as well as a comfortable, natural setting that facilitates maintenance of the parent–child relationship.

Parental conditions

In some instances, the maltreatment of children directly arises from a parental condition that alters the parents' ability to care for or protect their child. The parents' mental health or chemical dependence may directly contribute to neglectful or abusive behaviours that endanger the child and that cannot be controlled without appropriate, sometimes lengthy, treatment. Poor physical health may also result in limitations or an inability to parent adequately.

Here, the management of the condition so that parents can resume responsibility for their children's care may be the primary goal, rather than preparation for parenting. In some instances, particularly during the initial phase of placement, visits will necessarily be planned in collaboration with the parents' treatment staff. Clinicians may want to postpone, limit, or even increase visits, based on the projected effects of visits on the parents' treatment. You will need to weigh their concerns against the children's need for contact and reassurance that they have not been abandoned, and an assessment of what the child can cope with.

As parents demonstrate a level of recovery from physical or mental illness or chemical dependence that allows them to resume parenting, you should consider the amount of time they spend with their child and the degree of stress that they can successfully manage. Monitoring the parents' compliance with their treatment programme, such as regularly taking medication or attending Alcoholics Anonymous, is the key to child protection when ability to parent depends on the control or management of a diagnosed condition.

Imprisonment of a parent

Children are sometimes looked after when a custodial parent is imprisoned and arrangements with other appropriate carers, such as extended family members, cannot be made. When a parent's imprisonment is related to having harmed the child, the impact of contact with the parent on the child should be assessed. When family reunification is the goal, every effort should be made to assure regular visiting. The child's fantasy of the parent's experience in prison may be much more frightening than the reality, and visits can reassure the child that the parent is alive and safe.

In planning visits between children and imprisoned parents, it is essential to determine in advance what is required to secure permission for the child to visit, who can accompany the child to visits, and how often and for how long the child can visit. In order to appropriately prepare the child, you need to determine whether a child will be able to hug or kiss the parent or will be required to talk to the parent through a glass window, and what rules govern visit behaviour.

It is essential to examine your own attitudes about the child's visiting in prison. If you are uncomfortable with this plan, you may be depriving families of their right to contact by delaying the arrangement of visits.

Parents' compliance with visiting plans

The extent of the parents' compliance with the visiting plan must be considered. As emphasised earlier, visits are not planned to reward or punish parents for their co-operation or lack of it, but visit planning must take the parents' compliance into account.

Noncompliance may be examined at two levels: the actual behaviour and the meaning of the behaviour. Depending on the persistence and meaning of the noncompliance, your responses may differ. For example, parents might not co-operate with a plan for weekly visits at home, often not being there or always being late when the child is brought for the visits. This behaviour might indicate an inability to keep track of the visit schedule, ambivalence about visits in the home and family reunification, worry about their own ability to care for or protect the child in the home, reaction to the pain of being separated from the child, lack of interest in the child's return, and so forth. Each explanation suggests different actions for you to take.

Perhaps more common are parents who fail to turn up for visits in the office or other neutral place. Although this noncompliance might reflect lack of interest in the child or severe deficits in self-management, it could well be attributed to practical problems or extreme discomfort at simply being in that situation. Office visits are awkward under the best of circumstances, and this awkwardness is increased when, as is the case in many places, the visiting room is sterile and poorly furnished.

The reasons for lack of compliance with visit arrangements should always be explored. The lack of compliance might be due to problems with money, transport, or child care; inability to tell the time; changes in parents' work schedules; discomfort with the degree of responsibility given to them for the child's care; or simply misunderstanding of the arrangements. Eliminating such obstacles should always be tried before visit arrangements are modified.

When you determine that the apparent lack of co-operation is not the result of unreasonable expectations imposed by the agency or factors beyond the parents' control, and efforts to gain parental co-operation are unsuccessful, modifications in visit arrangements may be indicated. For example, if parents are consistently unavailable for visits in their home, a condition might be added to the visit plan requiring that they telephone to confirm that they are at home before the child is brought to the visit. Or, for a period of time, visits may be alternately scheduled in the foster home or at a location such as a park or cafe, where the parents' failure to be consistently available has less impact on the use of agency resources, such as travelling time, and where the child can be appropriately occupied while waiting.

When parents repeatedly fail to keep scheduled visits without good cause and despite your efforts to encourage visiting, a conference should be convened to discuss the visiting plan. It may seem useful to continue to arrange visits that parents are unlikely to keep simply to build up evidence on which to argue the case for termination of contact. Before this course of action is taken, however, the staff must consider its effect on the children. To look forward week after week to seeing parents who do not appear can be devastating to children who are strongly attached to their parents. Because of the serious legal and psychological consequences of decision making at this point, the agency must ensure that all relevant people are involved either by being present at a meeting or by having their opinions sought. Factual evidence which supports opinions should be fully recorded.

Parents' past endangering behaviours

In some instances, you will have access to information regarding parents' visit-related behaviours during a previous placement. This information may be pertinent, particularly during the initial assessment phase. To illustrate: when records indicate that during a visit parents have tried to abduct a child; have threatened or tried to harm the child, agency staff members, substitute carers, or others; have been dishonest about harm that occurred during a visit; or have failed to ask for help when they recognised that they were in over their heads, the visit plan should include prohibitions against these behaviours, and arrangements to prevent them. Moreover, visit location, supervision, and participants should be planned to maximise the protection of all involved. Agency supervisory staff should be involved in determining all visit arrangements in such cases.

Parents' wishes and requests

Considering parents' requests about arrangements for visits differs from developing a plan that provides for visits "at the parent's request". A plan that leaves parents to request visits one at a time usually results in less frequent visiting than a plan that outlines a pattern of visit arrangements. Plans for visits solely at the parent's request are therefore discouraged. They ignore parents' and children's rights to contact as well as the role of planned visits in the treatment process. Only when the goal is not reunification, such as preparation for independent living, should such a plan be considered.

It is essential that parents' preferences about contact arrangements be solicited and seriously considered. Solicited is a key word, as many parents hesitate to state their preferences. Parents may feel powerless and doubt your willingness to seriously consider their preferences; they may worry about rocking the boat and feel that their requests would result in less contact with their children. Don't assume that a lack of stated preferences reflects either a lack of motivation and interest in seeing their child, or agreement with the plan.

With parents, as with children, exploring the reason behind a request or stated preference is essential, since responding to the stated request may not effectively address the concern that prompted it. For example, one young mother requested that visits to her two children continue in the foster carers' home rather than be moved to her home as had been planned. Exploration revealed that she anticipated that when visits began in her home, her mother and sister would be critical of her care of the children and would take over, in contrast with the supportive way the foster carers had responded to her progress with the children. An intermediate step was planned. Two more visits were arranged in the foster home, with the mother's own mother, sister, and the social worker participating. This provided a chance for the mother's family to observe the improvements in her care of the children as well as to observe the social worker's and foster carers' support. The visits also allowed for open discussion of the expectations of the mother and her family when the visits shifted to the family's home.

Parents' reactions to visits

Visits evoke a range of reactions in parents. "Visiting" is typically thought of as making a social call by appointment. The idea of visiting one's own child, or having one's child visiting at home, stirs deep feelings for parents about themselves, their child, the substitute carers, and you, the social worker. For example, a young mother of a four-year-old girl who had been in foster care for about six months described her reactions in this way: 'I count the days to the next visit, but it rips my heart out to see her. She sees me as Mighty Mouse, thinking I can take her home, thinking I can make it happen, and I can't make it happen. It's hard not to be able to do what your child thinks you can.' A father angrily described his reactions to visits: 'There is never enough time. I dread coming. They make it hard on parents. They have all the power.' Parents experience vulnerability, anger, and sadness, and are reminded of their failure as parents. Your empathy for parents and sensitivity to their feelings as a "visiting" parent will help you determine which arrangements are most comfortable.

Sometimes, parents' reactions to visiting distress the children and may also affect you, such as when parents promise repeatedly that they will take their child home the next time they see him or her, or when parents are unwilling to end the goodbye embraces with their toddler. Whether you are disappointed, frustrated, or sympathetic in relation to parents, you must focus on their reaction, its meaning, and its impact on the child. Acknowledge the awkwardness, the pain, the discouragement, and the ambivalence that parents feel as they visit. Encourage them to talk with each other, with you, and with their therapists about their reactions to visits and how best to deal with their feelings.

When parents experience distress about ending visits and the separation following visits, an increase in visit frequency and duration should be considered as one way to relieve their distress. Extreme discomfort for parents visiting in the foster home, for example, may ultimately lead to making a change in visit arrangements. Before doing so, however, other interventions should be tried. Perhaps the foster mother is talking at length with a mother at each visit about the child's progress and success. The foster mother and the parent may hold radically different perceptions of this interaction. The mother may feel that the remarks are an implied criticism and infer disapproval; the foster mother may perceive the remarks as an important way to keep the mother informed about the child. In such instances, clarifying the perceptions and intentions may increase the foster carer's sensitivity and decrease the parent's discomfort.

It is realistic to expect that parents refrain from expressing their reactions inappropriately or in a manner hurtful to their children. When efforts to help them react appropriately are unsuccessful, the visiting plan should be revised either by identifying unacceptable behaviour in the plan or by revising the other aspects of the plan.

Parents' schedules and accessibility
It is often difficult to find a visiting time that is convenient for all involved. Finding a time when parents are not working and can get child

care, if necessary, for children at home, and arranging the visit at a place easily accessible to the parents must be high priorities. If parents work on a shift basis, arrangements will have to be flexible. Some parents, however, are either not employed, or have employment which allows them to take time off to see their child. It is useful to talk directly to parents about visiting as both a right and a responsibility, emphasising the importance of visiting for their child, for themselves, and as a part of the care plan. Making time for visits and use of other services must be a priority for parents during the placement period if children are to return home.

Parents sometimes move house and added distance becomes a major obstacle to regular, frequent visiting. At other times, the agency must place children at a distance from the parents. You and the parents should make every effort to continue visits as frequently as transport can be arranged. Visits should be supplemented with regular phone calls and letters.

Distance may also present an obstacle to visiting when parents are in prison. Some areas have volunteers who assist family members of inmates with arrangements and transport.

As discussed in Chapter 1, the agency's office hours may present a barrier to frequent visiting for some families. If you are finding this to be true, you should keep a record of the families whose need for visits at a specific time conflicts with agency hours. This information is necessary to press successfully for a change in the agency's practice or for another alternative service, such as increased use of volunteers and increased payment for transport.

Family relationships and interactions

The visit plan is also shaped by the relationships of persons visiting together and by the nature of their interactions. Family is broadly defined to include people living in the parent's household and acting as a member of the child's family, as well as those people related to the child. People viewed by the child as family, whether or not the relationship is legally sanctioned by marriage or by adoption, should be included, at least periodically, in visits.

The assessment of family relationships and interactions helps decide what frequency, length, and focus of visiting are necessary to maintain or build these relationships; what degree of structure, including monitoring or supervising visits and selecting visit activities, is necessary to maintain a safe, manageable level of stress and conflict during visits; what groupings of family members for visits will support the focus on parent–child interaction; and what natural resources are available for assistance with transport and supervision.

What visit arrangements will help maintain or build family relationships?
As discussed previously, maintaining and building family relationships constitutes a fundamental purpose of visiting, whatever the placement phase. The child's age and sense of time strongly suggest the minimum visit frequency necessary to maintain these relationships for the child. When parents and children do not know each other well, do not like each other, or have an ambivalent relationship, visits should be planned with sufficient flexibility to allow an uncomfortable visit to end early or a good time to last longer. When children are getting to know a parent who has been absent, including someone else with the child in the visit whom the child already knows and trusts, such as an older sibling or foster carer, may provide important security.

Relationships among family members have been damaged in many cases by the experiences they have shared. When children consistently avoid physical or eye contact with a family member, seek distance from him or her, or convey discomfort in other ways, do not try to force hugs, sitting on laps, or other affectionate gestures during visits. Children must be allowed to rebuild relationships at their own pace. Parents may need your assistance in understanding this.

What visiting options will assure a safe, manageable level of stress and conflict?
The degree of conflict among members of the parents' household, divorced parents, or the extended family may sometimes limit your visiting options. Although conflict is definitely neither always negative nor always predictable, when there is reason to believe that family conflicts have the potential to escalate into emotional assault or physical

violence, or when children are pulled into arguments among adults, visits should minimise that possibility. Consider selecting a more restrictive venue for the visits, or having the agency supervise the visits, or arranging separate visits for disputing parties. To illustrate:

John's uncle lived in John's parents' home, helped with child care, and was close to John. Soon after John was placed, his father and uncle got into a fight that caused serious injuries to both, and John's uncle moved out. John wanted to see both his uncle and dad, and separate visits were planned. In another example, a mother who was wheelchair-bound was accompanied by her mother to the first two visits with her children. During each visit, the grandmother harshly criticised her daughter's care of the children to the point where the mother dissolved into tears. After discussing the situation, the social worker and the mother planned several visits at a time when the mother's sister, who was more supportive, could accompany her. In the interim period, the mother and grandmother agreed to meet with a family therapist to work on their conflictual relationship and its effect on the mother's parenting.

When it is evident that the combinations of family members involved in visiting create conflict and stress, you should consider a time-limited change in visiting arrangements to provide relief. For example, perhaps a mother with three sons in placement who is unable to manage her two older sons' teasing and taunting of her youngest son could visit the youngest and his siblings separately, for several visits. This would allow her to attend to her relationship with her youngest son without the constant distraction and conflict created by the older boys' behaviour. In such cases, counselling concerning the conflict should be provided. Conflict that is not addressed will be likely to continue and to affect the success of reunification.

What arrangements will increase the focus on parent–child interaction?
A focus on parent–child interaction during visits supports the primary purpose of visits, maintaining the parent–child relationship. You must be alert for instances where parent–child interactions are not the focus of visiting. For example, parents often ask to include a relative, boy/girlfriend, neighbour, or friend in visits. Is dad bored during visits and therefore brings along a friend? Does mum want her mother to come

along to do the work of caring for a fractious baby? Or is dad bringing a friend who will join him in playing with his son? Is mum bringing her mother to show off her new-found ability to take care of her child?

Answers to questions such as these are critical, for children in placement fear abandonment and worry about rejection or that mum and dad will forget them. When their parents' attention during visits is consistently and primarily focused on someone else, children's self-esteem and sense of worth suffer.

Parents may also concentrate on one or two of their children to the exclusion of others – on the most troublesome child, the most verbal, or the youngest. Your knowledge of the family will help you decide whether, with your help, the parents can spread their attention more broadly; or whether, for a period of time, parents should visit their children individually or in subgroups so that each child can share in the parents' attention.

Parents often interact with their children as if the latter were their peers, partners, or parents. A parent may burden the child with a list of problems and question: 'What should I do? How can I manage without you?' When this happens, help the parent interact with the child more appropriately during visits by identifying the interactions as problematic, by helping the parent plan child-centered activities, and, if necessary, arranging for someone to supervise the visits. Services should also be addressing the problem of parent–child role reversal.

How can the family's social support network be tapped?

Parents may have friends or relatives who can help with transport. Moreover, reliable relatives or friends may be sufficiently concerned about a child's well-being to supervise visits in their home or in the parents' home, with a clear agreement as to their role and responsibilities. This option is particularly useful during the latter part of the central phase and the reunification phase, when the parents' progress has decreased the risk to the child.

Friends and relatives can help parents care for their children during visits in the parents' home and reinforce parents in the parenting role. Although a friend or relative should not assume all or even primary responsibility for child care, we all know that parents in general often rely on friends and relatives for help with supervision and care and for advice and support. Why should we expect parents whose children are being looked after to assume sole responsibility during home visits? In fact, learning how to develop and use support networks appropriately is a major task of many parents whose children are in placement.

5 Specific considerations: the foster carers

This chapter includes guidelines for determining how foster carers might be involved in visits. In residential care, the visiting plan will be influenced more by the policies of the establishment than by your assessment of the substitute carers.

Agencies differ in their capacity to support foster carers' involvement in visits. Foster carers also differ significantly in their capacity and willingness to have contact with parents and to carry out different roles in visiting. Although foster carers cannot be allowed to determine whether children and parents will visit, they can influence the nature of the contact that can take place between them and parents and the decision about where visits will take place.

Agency capacity to support foster carers' involvement in visiting

An essential consideration in planning visits is the amount of support the agency can provide to foster carers. Depending on the agency's assessment, preparation and training practices and the foster carers' experiences with the agency, foster carers' definitions of their role may vary. Where agencies see foster carers as team members who join with social workers and others in working towards a child's return home, foster carers are likely to define their role to include extensive personal contact with the child's family, and to have developed the capacity to do so. The opposite is true in agencies that do not define foster caring in this way. The assessment of carer capacity for involvement with visits therefore covers not only individual capacity but also the agency's past and current contribution to the development of that capacity. If many of the children in your case load are placed with foster carers who do not define involvement with the child's family as part of the foster carer's role, changes in the agency's foster carer recruitment, approval, and training programme and in the agency's approach to partnership with carers are probably indicated.

A number of questions can be asked to assess your agency's support of foster carers' involvement in visiting. Can the agency reimburse foster carers for the costs of transport and child care? Does the agency provide groups for foster carers where they have opportunities to learn and to share experiences with other foster carers? Do you have the time to listen to foster carers' concerns and to provide consultation and emotional support? If the answer to these questions is "yes", foster carers can be actively involved in visiting. If the agency cannot support foster carers' involvement in visiting, it is not reasonable to expect them to be active participants.

Foster carers' capacity to support reunification

Some foster carers can and should have extensive personal contact with the parents of a child who is in their care. Other foster carers, however, cannot work effectively with a child's parents and should have very limited contact. Your answers to the following questions will help you to determine foster carers' capacity to be involved in visiting.

What are the foster carers' attitudes towards parents?

While not necessarily condoning a particular parent's behaviour, do the foster carers accept parents as persons and understand the stress they feel? Foster carers who accept children's parents can be helpful to parents; non-accepting carers can undermine parents' confidence and efforts to change. If carers look after children from a different cultural or racial background than the carers, they may need help in understanding cultural values and needs.

Do the foster carers value the child–parent relationship?

Foster carers who recognise and appreciate the importance of parents to their children will be able to share a child and to support the relationship between a child and his or her parents. Foster carers who do not value this relationship are likely to compete with parents and to undermine improvement in the child's relationship with the parents. Contact between such foster carers and the child's parents must be closely monitored.

Can the foster carers appropriately limit their relationship with the child's parents?

Foster carers must be able to differentiate their role from that of the parents' social worker. It is not appropriate for them to try to counsel the child's parents or to make assurances to parents about the outcome of placement. Foster carers who are confident in their role as substitute carers and are able to restrict their relationship with parents consistent with this role will manage contact without agency supervision.

Can the foster carers objectively record visit interactions?

Foster carers should be encouraged to record actual interactions without allowing their own feelings about the parents and the children to interfere. In some instances, they may need assistance in exploring why they seem to emphasise parents' lack of progress one-sidedly. Foster carers who can objectively observe and record interactions can be a valuable resource for supervising visits.

Can the foster carers intervene as necessary?

Some foster carers are assertive and able to intervene with parents as needed. Others are fearful and hesitant in their interactions with parents. To illustrate: parents who abuse alcohol may have as a condition of visiting that they be sober during visits. If a foster carer is comfortable in refusing to allow a parent who appears to be intoxicated to take a child from the foster home for a visit, the plan can allow the parent to pick the child up at the foster home. If a foster parent is not comfortable saying "no", arrangements must be made to have someone else present when the parent meets the child.

Will the foster carers maintain confidentiality?

All foster carers are expected to hold confidential any information concerning children and their parents. People differ, however, in their ability to do this. Moreover, visiting raises some special issues concerning confidentiality. Visiting is both a public and private event. Not everything that occurs during a visit should be reported to you. Family conversations that do not relate to the plan for the child or reflect progress or lack of progress need not be repeated to you. As the placement continues, much of the interaction between child and parents can, and should, be private. Two questions, therefore, that arise in determining whether foster carers can supervise visits or be involved in visits are firstly, can they resist sharing information with persons outside the agency and secondly, can they discern what you should be told and what can remain private?

What are the foster carers' resources?

Visiting is demanding on all participants and can be costly in terms of time and physical and emotional energy. The extent to which foster carers can be involved in visiting depends in part on their resources. Do they have the time to provide transport? Do they have the time to supervise visits or to teach parenting skills during visits? Do they have the physical and emotional energy to be involved frequently with children's parents?

The answers to these questions reflect not only the foster carers' characteristics, but also the demands imposed on them. If foster carers have only one child, or the children from only one family, in placement, they will have more resources to devote to contact. If they are caring for children from more than one family, their resources will be spread more thinly. They cannot be as helpful with visits, as much as you and they might want.

Some situations are less demanding than others. If the case is unusually difficult, for whatever reason, the foster carers' resources will be more quickly strained; they may not be able to be as actively involved in visiting as you might wish.

Money is a resource that is often overlooked in considering how foster carers might be involved in visiting. Agencies usually reimburse foster carers for the costs they incur in support of visiting. It is a problem when agencies do not reimburse foster carers for these expenses or when foster carers have to wait for several weeks to be reimbursed. This problem can be significant when visits are frequent and the distances are great.

Can the foster carers be flexible and tolerate stress?

Parents of children in placement are often disorganised and unpredictable. The extent to which foster carers can manage this will determine in part the extent to which they can be involved in visiting.

Can the foster carers recognise their need for assistance?

Visiting stirs complex feelings in foster carers, particularly at the beginning of placement when they may feel outrage at how a child has been treated, and as the time for reunification nears when they are confronted with feelings of loss. Moreover, events occur in visits that may necessitate a request for the agency's assistance. The extent to which foster carers can interact personally with parents before, during and after visits without your involvement will be influenced by their ability to request assistance appropriately and to use the assistance and consultation that you provide.

Foster carers' willingness to assist with visiting

It is evident that foster carers' unwillingness to assist with visiting may affect their usefulness as a placement resource. A foster carer's willingness to assist with visiting should, therefore, be considered in approval and placement matching decisions. Some foster carers have personal qualities that could make them a valuable resource in working towards reunification, but for a variety of reasons, are unwilling to be involved in visiting in certain ways.

All foster carers should be expected to help prepare the child for visits and to fit in with reasonable visiting plans. Foster carer applicants who are not willing to do so should not be approved. Unless there is agency policy to the contrary, however, foster carers have the right to refuse to allow visits in their home and to refuse to supervise visits or to teach parenting skills during visits. You therefore need to assess the foster carers' willingness to allow visits in their home; to supervise visits in their home or elsewhere, and to record what occurs as requested; and to teach a parent how to provide special care that the child might need.

When you discover after a child has been placed that foster carers are unwilling to be involved in visiting, you should initially assume an educational role. Describe the purposes of visiting, stress the importance of the foster carers' commitment to visiting, and reassess with them what they are willing to do. If the foster carers then modify their reactions and agree to reasonable visiting plans, other resources should be sought to supplement their involvement. If, after further discussion they are still unwilling to be involved in visiting, it is unlikely they will be supportive of other reunification efforts. Disruption of the placement must then be considered.

Foster family's schedule

The visiting plan must also take the foster family's schedule into account. If a foster carer will need to comfort a child following a visit, the plan must assure that he or she is home when the child returns from a visit, rather than have the child returned by a parent or a volunteer at a time when it is known that a foster carer will not be home and an older child or someone else will be receiving the child. Similarly, beginnings and endings of visits should not be fixed at times that will be highly disruptive for the foster family, such as the family's regular dinner hour.

Visits at weekends or holiday times require particularly thoughtful advance planning in order to minimise confusion for the child and disruption to the foster family.

Impact of visiting on other children in the home

A final consideration related to the foster family is the impact of visiting on other children in the home. As in the case of foster carers' capacity and willingness to participate in visiting, the impact on other children cannot preclude visits but it may influence the place where visits take place and other arrangements.

How distressing are one child's visits to other children in the foster home?

Many foster carers look after children from more than one family at a time. Moreover, many foster carers have biological children and many have adopted former foster children. One child's visits can have a powerful effect on other children in the family, either foster, adopted, or biological. One child's visits may generate both positive and negative reminders for other children of their own parents. It is easy to overlook the effect of one child's visits on other children in the home. If visiting in the foster home or if contact between the foster family and one child's parents appears to be having a detrimental effect on another child, consideration must be given to changing arrangements.

Does support of one child's visits result in neglect of other children in the home?

In their desire to be helpful, foster carers may commit themselves to more than they can realistically do. They may not recognise the signs of overcommitment until it is too late – until they become impatient with all the children in the home or until a child in the home manifests new problematic behaviour. When they recognise that they cannot give sufficient attention to one child because of the demands that another child imposes, they may not tell you out of fear that you will think they are inadequate and will move a child. You must be alert to the balance of attention the children are receiving and make other visiting arrangements if it appears that one child's visiting plan is resulting in lack of attention to other children in the home.

6 Preparing for and co-ordinating visits

When you have a contact plan that is closely related to the care plan and goals, and takes the specifics of the child's situation into account, your task is well begun but, in a sense, just half-done. The plan that you have carefully developed or recently revised is not likely to be followed unless you are actively involved in preparing the child, family members, and substitute carers for visits, in co-ordinating visiting arrangements, and in continually evaluating the visits that take place. This chapter discusses these tasks as well as the documentation of visits.

Questions for all persons involved in visiting

All persons directly involved in visiting should have complete, current information about visiting arrangements and regular opportunities to talk about visiting and the feelings stirred by visiting. Each person should also have regular opportunities to discuss the following explicit questions with you.

What is the current contact plan?

This includes information about the frequency, length, and location of visits, and whether and by whom they will be supervised. Who will participate in arrangements for transport, activities during visits, required or prohibited behaviours, and how changes in visiting arrangements can be made must also be addressed. The plan will also include arrangements for contact between visits.

How is everyone likely to react to visits?

We all find it useful to know what to expect when we are facing a difficult situation. This is certainly true with visiting, an event that for most parents and children is initially extremely awkward and emotionally charged. Knowing something about typical responses to visits can help participants prepare for and cope with their own reactions. The result will be more rewarding and productive visits. For example, parents who know that during the early part of visits many children act as if they are angry with their parents or shy away from their parents are more likely to cope with this behaviour than parents who expect children to respond warmly.

Because feelings concerning placement and visiting are intense, it may be tempting to avoid discussing common negative reactions to visits, to reassure those involved that "everything will be okay". Everything during visits may not be okay, and certainly most children and their families will not be feeling okay, particularly early in the placement. Such statements, therefore, fail to convince family members. Moreover, because these reassurances have no foundation they may not only be misleading, but also block effective communication between you and family members. They may also undermine the parent–child relationship by creating false expectations and disappointment.

What is expected of me during visits?

Clarify the role and responsibilities of each person and discuss planned activities. This decreases the awkwardness of visits and increases the likelihood that activities will contribute to progress in the plan. Part of your responsibility is to teach family members and others what is expected of them and how best to make visits meaningful and purposeful.

What are the options for handling problems related to visiting?

Most people, at least at some point in the process, have worries and fears about visiting: What if she doesn't return him on time? What if he acts up and won't do what he is told? What if my mum leaves me? The list of "what if?" questions can be lengthy. Identifying and thinking through the "what if?" questions may decrease anxiety and, more importantly, may enable participants to prevent difficult or dangerous situations or to handle them should they occur.

Whenever possible, you, the parents, older children, and the substitute carers should meet together to review arrangements and responsibilities and expectations. Discussion with all persons involved may prevent misunderstandings and problems. Should problems arise later, this discussion, especially if recorded, serves as a point of reference and helps in confronting "no one told me" complaints.

Working with children

Immediately following placement, or before placement if the placement has been planned, the questions listed above should be discussed with children. In the initial phase of the placement, preparing children for visiting should focus on their anxieties and fears about being with their parents and the limits on contact that are imposed. Must they stay in the room? Will they not see someone they expect to see? Recognise that it is normal for children to be nervous, ambivalent, and confused about visiting, and preoccupied with details. Who will pick me up? Where will it be? Will I be home for lunch? Since younger children have difficulty with time, the days of the week and phrases such as "for an hour" have little meaning. Use instead the child's understanding of routine, such as before or after lunch, while Sesame Street is on, or on the day Billy and Susie don't go to school. Providing an individual calendar with visiting days marked helps school-age children keep track of the visiting schedule.

Help children become aware of their feelings and talk about them. You might say something like 'Some children feel nervous and some are really excited. How about you?' Or 'Some children get upset when they say goodbye when visits end, but some children are glad.' Or 'After visiting, some children feel angry or lonely. It helps to talk about your feelings.' Where a child's concern for personal safety can be anticipated, describe what the person supervising the visit will do if necessary to protect the child.

Whenever possible, elicit the child's fantasy of what visiting will be like, then correct misinformation, respond to feelings, and think through the "what if?" questions together. Using play or drawings to help children communicate their ideas and feelings about visiting is often useful. You might use dolls to illustrate a fictional story about children in placement who visit their parents, describing important things such as place, participants, the role of the visit supervisor, and the children's worries and reactions. You and the child might read a book together about a child in placement. Or you might ask children to draw pictures of what they imagine visiting will be like, what they wish it would be like, or what they are worried it will be like, and use the drawings as a means for the children to talk about their fantasies and questions.

Children are often reassured to know that other children are in foster care and visiting their parents and that these children have many of the same reactions to visits. Encouraging discussion about visiting among siblings in placement or among a group of several children recently placed decreases each child's sense of isolation and of being different and may prompt discussion about concerns that children might not have brought up individually.

As the placement progresses into the central and reunification phases, preparing for visits occurs alongside the processing and evaluation of previous visits. What happened? How did it feel? What should continue the same? What should be changed? In most instances the child's preparation for visits during these phases also occurs in discussions with the child's carer and play therapist.

As agency supervision of visits decreases, discuss thoroughly with the child the indicators that a visiting situation might be becoming volatile or dangerous. Develop a plan that the child can follow should she or he need to call for help or get away from the situation. Practice the required skills, such as dialing the number where you or other designated persons will be available to the child. Developing the child's age-appropriate self-care and protection skills is an essential aspect of visit preparation as reunification approaches.

If it is decided that family reunification is not possible, children need assistance in understanding the alternative permanent plan, why they cannot return home, and the nature of the relationships they will have with family members in the future. The child will need your help in dealing with the reality of changing or ending family relationships and with any resulting changes in contact. Children must know when contact with their parents and other family members will be limited or ended. Help them plan what they would like to do, say, or ask in final visits. Explore what would support them in coping with these vital happenings in their lives. What is not worked through now will handicap their emotional growth.

Working with family members

Parents must also have regular opportunities to explore the four questions set forth earlier in this chapter. In the initial phase of the placement, the preparation of parents should also cover several additional areas. First, stress how important parents are to their children. Initially after placement, many parents feel blamed and worthless or defensive. A clear message as to their value and importance to their children is both affirming and encouraging.

Second, discuss the pull to avoid visiting that many parents experience because of the awkwardness, anger, numbness, or sadness they feel or expect to feel upon seeing their child. Ways to deal with feelings and reactions other than avoiding visits should be discussed.

Third, emphasise parents' rights and responsibilities with regard to visiting. Describe the agency's intention to provide regular, frequent visiting and the parents' and child's right to it. Strongly emphasise parents' responsibility to visit. Discuss the insult children experience when their parents do not visit and children's fears of being abandoned by their parents. Make clear that visiting is the principal means for parents to protect their relationship with their child during placement and that visiting has a central role in your work with them towards the child's return home. Moreover, parents must be informed explicitly of the possible legal consequences of their failure to visit. In other words, help parents understand how necessary visiting is and convey a clear, non-ambiguous message: you expect the parents to visit and will work with them to develop and carry out a visiting plan.

Fourth, prepare parents for their children's behaviour during visits, such as clinging and crying or anger and withdrawal; reassure parents that many children in placement, not just theirs, behave in unpredictable ways during visits, and provide suggestions about handling these behaviours.

Fifth, spell out the various functions that persons supervising visits may have, including helping parents to learn to deal with children's behaviour, recording changes and progress in the family interactions, and setting limits on behaviours that could become hurtful. Make sure that the parents know that the visit supervisor will report to you concerning what he or she observes.

Finally, when germane, make clear the agency's and the court's expectations that the parents will not pressurise children to recant their allegations of abuse, and identify any other visit-related behaviour that the agency has concluded must be required or prohibited in each case.

As the placement progresses, working with parents on visiting increasingly involves evaluating previous visits and planning subsequent ones. Planning visit activities suited to the child's current developmental tasks, as described in Chapter 3, allows for teaching and for emphasising the importance of parent–child interactions during visits.

When parents do not visit as arranged, it is essential that you contact them immediately to determine why the appointment was not kept. This is consistent with your statement to them that you expect them to fulfill their responsibility to visit. Re-emphasise the importance of visiting for their child's well-being and for reunification. Identify any obstacles to visiting that may exist and explore any reactions the parents have to visiting that may be affecting their compliance with the plan.

Throughout the placement, working with parents on visiting addresses the parents' feelings about each child in placement and about the plan for reunification. Your attention to parents' reactions to visits and to preparing parents for visits and evaluating visits is essential. Discussions with parents about their visits and the assessment of the feasibility and timing of the child's return home are closely related. Be watchful for indications of parental ambivalence about reunification so that worries, questions, and feelings can be explored. In some instances, sensitive exploration of ambivalence may over time lead to a parent's decision that the child should not return home.

People other than parents who visit, including nonplaced siblings and unrelated members of the parents' household, should also be prepared for visiting. Explain the purposes of visiting and the expectation that during visits the parents are responsible for their children's care and supervision. Specify that visiting family members are expected to support, not interfere with, the parents' involvement with their child.

Working with foster carers and other substitute carers
Foster carers are usually with their foster children before and after each visit and, in many instances, visits are held at the child's placement and

monitored by the foster carers. Continuing discussions with substitute carers about visiting are vital. As noted in the introduction to this guide, the majority of children in placement are cared for by foster carers, but substitute carers also include relatives providing placement and staff members in residential homes. Although we refer primarily to foster carers in this section, the discussion applies to all persons providing substitute care.

Like children and parents, all carers need regular opportunities to discuss the following questions:

What is the current visiting plan?

What can I expect in terms of my own and other's reactions to visiting?

What should I do during visits? What is expected of me?

How should I handle visit-related problems? What are my options if I need assistance?

Unlike children and parents, foster carers may have had opportunities to review in training sessions the purposes of visiting and their involvement in visiting. Some carers have had extensive training or experience with visiting. In these instances, your discussions can focus primarily on the plan for the particular child and family, how the foster carers will help carry out the plan, and the reactions and questions that they have.

If the foster carers have not participated in training or if they have had previous negative experiences with visiting, you will have more work to do with them. Describe the purposes of visiting and stress the importance of the foster carers' commitment to visiting. You may want to enlist a foster carer who has had positive experiences with visiting as a resource or consultant to the foster carers during the child's placement. If your agency does not provide training and reading materials on visiting for foster carers, you may want to discuss the need for this with your supervisor and with other agency staff members.

You should help carers think about visiting from the child's and parents' points of view. Discuss together what you both might do to decrease their discomfort. For example, if several visits are to be located in the foster carers' home, what would best facilitate natural interaction between parent and child; encourage parental responsibility for the child's care and supervision during the visit; and provide appropriate privacy?

When visits are held elsewhere and the parent is coming for the child, should the foster carer walk the child to the car or invite the parent to come in? What should be ready for the child to take to visits away from the foster home, for example, clothes? Toys?

As noted in Chapter 5, foster caters may assume different roles and responsibilities with regard to visiting depending on the care plan; the child's needs; the parents' feelings, attitudes, and behaviours; and the foster carers' capacity, skills, training, and attitudes. In support of visiting, however, all foster carers are expected to:

- co-operate with the visiting plan, sometimes assisting with transport, recording visit-related information, and sometimes permitting the child to spend special days with parents;
- encourage the child's open expression of feelings about visiting;
- maintain confidentiality about the child and the child's family;
- avoid demeaning the parents and other relatives to the child or to others;
- discuss their own reactions to visiting arrangements with you, not with the child or parents.

In most cases, visits at some point during the placement will be held in the foster home. Other activities in which both the parents and the foster carers may participate would include school conferences, clinic appointments, and so forth. In many cases foster carers will provide additional services, such as helping parents develop parenting skills through teaching and role-modelling. Whatever the agreement regarding the foster carers' role and responsibilities in visiting, your availability to them to plan, process, advise, interpret, and mediate is essential to the plan's success. Foster carers must be encouraged to identify and record progress that they observe. Problems that arise should be dealt with quickly and directly.

In your discussion with foster carers regarding visiting, try to anticipate the problems that might arise and discuss possible responses. Foster carers should be encouraged to contact you, or if appropriate an out-of-hours social worker, as soon as possible when:

- parents do not keep visiting appointments or try to visit at unscheduled times;
- parents come for visits late, very distressed, intoxicated, or with persons who don't have permission to visit;

- parents behave in ways that upset their child or other children in the home;
- parents refuse to end visits or consistently return the child from visits later than agreed;
- the child consistently tries to avoid visiting or ending visits;
- the child is distressed by visiting or some aspect of the visiting arrangements; or
- other observations suggest visit-related difficulties.

Much of the discussion up to this point suggests that the interaction between foster carers and a child's parents is always problematic, but foster carers who are committed to reunification and who view themselves as important agents in achieving reunification typically derive a great deal of satisfaction from their work with parents. Their contributions are often overlooked, however. They need and deserve your encouragement, recognition, and suggestions concerning their work.

Working with others who provide visit-related services

People providing visit-related services such as transport, interpreting, supervision, or individualised parent education also need adequate preparation to fulfill their responsibilities. It is important to provide sufficient information without adding case information that is not necessary to their role, and that might violate confidentiality.

People who transport family members to visits must have accurate information about time and place, best route, how long to wait, need for a child's or infant's car seat, most workable seating arrangements in the car for siblings, and anticipated behaviour management problems and methods to deal with them. It is important to develop a way of promptly getting the transporter's observations of the children and any other information that might affect subsequent visit planning.

People supervising visits need to know the particular purpose of their supervision. As discussed earlier, supervision, as we use the term, has many purposes. Is the purpose primarily child protection? Is the purpose to provide instruction? Does the supervisor need to assess the current functioning of a family member or the whole family? How important is documentation of the visiting interactions? Whatever the purpose, visit supervisors need information concerning the reason for placement and the care plan. They also need information about difficulties that may arise during the visit and preferred methods for resolving difficulties. They need to know under what circumstances visits should be ended prematurely and who will be available if assistance is needed. In addition, the agency's requirements for documentation should be spelled out and forms provided, if necessary. A plan for follow-up with persons supervising visits is essential so that you can have the benefit of their observations.

As in the case of foster carers, volunteers and professional staff members who provide visit-related services need and deserve recognition of their efforts and feedback concerning their work. This is particularly true regarding volunteers and family aides who, unlike professionally trained staff members, often lack confidence and are uncertain about how to evaluate their own performance. Moreover, volunteers receive no pay, and the salaries of family aides are typically very low. Your thanks and suggestions can be powerful motivators to keep them involved in providing services.

Co-ordinating and evaluating visiting arrangements

Co-ordination and evaluation of visiting arrangements are necessary to facilitate the harmonious working of all involved towards the same end. Co-ordination and evaluation include several responsibilities:

– development of the visiting plan;
– preparation for those involved for visits, including convening meetings of persons involved as necessary to clarify roles, expectations, and arrangements;
– provision of needed visit-related services such as transport or day care, or referral for such services;
– monitoring compliance of all parties with the visiting plan;
– monitoring the consistency between visit arrangements and agency policy and court orders;
– constant assessment of the appropriateness of the visiting plan given the current phase of work and progress;
– revision of the plan when necessary;
– mediation of conflicts that arise in relation to visiting;
– advocacy on behalf of children and families when obstacles to visiting are created by agency practices or when visit-related services to which

they are entitled are not available, not provided, or of poor quality; and
– assurance that an agency supervisor is aware of and involved in decision making related to visiting and is alerted to problems and difficulties that are expected or that occur unexpectedly.

To co-ordinate and evaluate visiting effectively, you will need first-hand knowledge of how the arrangements are being carried out. Even if other arrangements are available, providing transport or periodically monitoring visits yourself is necessary to evaluate not only the family's interaction but also how visiting arrangements are being carried out by substitute carers and other service providers. Meeting regularly with all the parties to visiting in a given case helps to exchange information, to identify and resolve problems, and to encourage appropriate changes in the plan. At a minimum, the plan must be reviewed with all participants as part of the regularly scheduled case review.

Documentation of visits

Because visiting is an essential element of the agency's service to families, accurate records must be maintained regarding the contact plan and its revisions, the family's involvement in visiting, and the related services provided. Most agencies require that substitute carers maintain a log recording visit dates, time of visits, participants, interactions they observe, and the child's reactions following the visit. Although all persons providing visit-related services have direct observations to record, it must be clear where and by whom the agency's official records of each child's visits are maintained. Many agencies have designed a form or logsheet to increase consistent recording of visit-related case information.

Another aspect of documentation is often overlooked – maintaining records concerning unmet needs and obstacles to visiting. If you are to identify service needs effectively and advocate on behalf of children and families served by your agency, it is necessary for you, your supervisor, and others in your agency to maintain a list of resources that are needed but cannot be provided, of agency placement practices that result in visit-related difficulties (such as distance of placement), and a record of the number of clients affected.

7 Support for the social worker

As described in Chapter 1, visits can place enormous stress on you. You observe the distress of children and parents. You may feel vulnerable professionally as you make judgements about the safety of children. You may feel personally vulnerable when parents become threatening or hostile. You may struggle to keep your professional and personal lives balanced as you find yourself arranging visits in your own time to accommodate parents' schedules, or find yourself preoccupied over the weekends or holidays with concern about children who are having extended visits at home.

If you are to maintain your commitment to visiting in the face of the demands it imposes and carry out this commitment competently, caring for yourself is vital. There are several types of stress-producing problems that, when recognised, can be ameliorated. These include failure to use fully those resources that are available to support your work related to visiting, difficulties in management of case load and time, and difficulties in recognising and asserting one's professional and personal limits. Suggestions concerning each of these are discussed briefly below.

Using available resources

Identify the resources your agency does provide to support your work in relation to visiting and ask yourself: am I using these resources to the fullest or carrying more of the load alone than is actually necessary? The resources include not only the persons available to provide visit-related services but also supervision, case conferences, and team meetings where visit plans and concerns can be reviewed and discussed. Most workers find that shared decision making reduces the sense of vulnerability and the stress that accompany difficult visit decisions. Sometimes workers hesitate to use case conferences or team meetings for fear of self-exposure, or of losing some of the autonomy they have in visit planning. The benefits, however, are substantial. Groups generate creative resolutions to problems and provide a broad base of information to draw from, as well as a shoulder to lean on.

Another agency resource that supports your work in visits is flexitime or time-off-in-lieu of overtime. The demands of planning, scheduling, and supervising visits while also meeting other appointments often make it seem as if your schedule is out of your hands and out of control. Take a look at your calendar for the past three months. Have you been using flexitime to adjust your professional schedule? Have you claimed allowable compensated time to balance out the additional visit-related work hours? Are you using your annual leave entitlement to detach yourself periodically from your work and replenish yourself? Or have you become resigned to losing time-off-in-lieu or part of your annual leave because you "don't have the time" to claim your time? Protecting your personal time and life by claiming the time benefits your agency provides is essential to self-care.

If your agency is short on supportive resources for visiting, identify those that are not provided and develop a strategy for obtaining them. For example, if your agency does not provide for flexibility in your work time to arrange visits according to clients' needs, begin to document the instances in which this has barred regular, frequent visiting and assert the need for this change on your clients' and your own behalf. Your supervisor and colleagues can be allies in documenting needs for visit-related services, for greater variation in agency hours, and for agency policies and practices that support visiting.

Management of case load and time

Allocation of work loads and poor time management also contribute to workers' stress levels. Review your case load with your supervisor. Is there variation within it (ages of children, permanency plans, reason for placement), or are you serving a homogenous case load with characteristics that present visit scheduling problems for you? For example, are many of your children placed at some distance from home? Are most of the children in your case load of school age, requiring after-school visits during the academic year? Variety within case loads contributes to greater flexibility in managing visits, particularly supervised visits, and decreases the cynicism or boredom that can be a reaction to carrying a full case load of similar cases.

Books and workshops on time management offer consistent advice to set priorities and use these to determine your daily schedule; to delegate; to set aside regular uninterrupted time periods for activities that require concentration; and to determine what investments in time will pay off in time saved. A time-management principle in visiting is that a heavy investment in time at the beginning for planning and preparation of persons involved will decrease problems and save time as the placement progresses. There are variations on this theme. For example, time spent in locating and preparing reliable, competent resource persons to provide visit transport or supervision is an investment that will free up your time for case activities that cannot be delegated, and free you from the concern that you will be forced to choose between assisting with a child's visit and dealing with a crisis in another case.

Recognising and asserting limits

Workers often contribute to their visit-related stresses by not recognising and asserting their own limits. Limitations involve not only schedule, but also some more personal in nature. For example, one stress-producing limit that must be recognised and confronted is that of professional expertise. You may feel insufficiently prepared to make the decisions described in this book, to prepare persons for visits, or to supervise specific visits. You have a right to expect your agency to provide orientation and training about your work and to provide a supervisor who is knowledgeable and available to discuss visit decisions and planning with you. In instances where supervision of visits could involve a risk to you, you have a right to supervisory involvement in developing a plan that protects you as well as your clients.

Another stress-producing limit is a temporary or persistent inability to cope with the steady exposure to intense feelings and reactions related to family relationships that visiting requires. If you have had or are in the midst of personal experiences rather like those of your clients, you may find yourself overidentifying with either parents or children in visiting situations, focusing on your own current situation or memories rather than on your clients' situations, thus under- or overinvesting in service to particular clients. If this is occurring, it is important to talk with your supervisor, a colleague, or a counsellor to sort out how your reactions or sensitivity to the clients' situations may be affecting your professional performance and your own well-being. Resolving personal matters directly rather than through your clients is a professional responsibility. In such instances a temporary shift in work responsibilities should be explored with your supervisor.

Workers often describe their attraction to the challenge, the importance, the pace, and the diversity of child care work. Stress is inherent, however, in this work generally, and is a constant factor in visit-related activities. No matter what support agencies provide, most workers experience periods of increased stress. It is necessary, therefore, to learn to monitor your own stress level and to use those methods of stress-reduction you find useful. There are many resources that describe the indicators which show when job-related stress is reaching a level that is affecting your well-being and performance. Recognising your own personal distress indicators and intervening on your own behalf is essential. You must care for yourself if you are to care for others.

Further reading

Ahmed S, Cheetham J, and Small J, eds, *Social Work with Black Children and their Families*, BAAF/Batsford, 1986.

Barber S, 'Planning Access for Children's Care', *Adoption & Fostering*, Vol 9 (3), 1985.

Bebbington A, Miles J, 'The Supply of Foster Families for Children in Care', *British Journal of Social Work*, 20, 1990.

Blumenthal K and Weinberg A, 'Issues Concerning Parental Visiting of Children in Foster Care' in *Foster Children in the Courts*, M Hardin (ed), Butterworth Legal Publishers, 1983, USA.

Fanshel D, and Shinn E, *Children in Foster Care: A longitudinal investigation*, Columbia University Press, 1978, USA.

Fratter J, 'Parties in the Triangle: Study of adopted children with contact', *Adoption & Fostering*, Vol 15 (4), 1991.

Fratter J, Rowe J, Sapsford D and Thoburn J, *Permanent Family Placement: A decade of experience*, BAAF, 1991.

Gilmour I, 'Parental Access in Scotland', *Adoption & Fostering*, Vol 10 (3), 1986.

Hess P, 'Case and Context: Determinants of Planned Visit Frequency in Foster Family Carer', *Child Welfare* LXVII, 4: 311-326, 1988 USA.

Hess P, Mintun G, Moelman A, and Pitts G, 'The Family Connection Center: An Innovative Visiting Program', *Child Welfare* LXXI, 1: 77-88, 1992, USA.

Hess P, and Proch K, 'How the States Regulate Parent-Child Visiting', *Public Welfare* 44, 4: 12-17, 1986, USA.

Hess P, and Proch K, 'Parent–Child Visiting Policies of Voluntary Agencies', *Children and Youth Services Review* 9 1: 17-18, 1987, USA.

Hess P, and Proch K, 'Visiting: The Heart of Reunification' in *Together Again:*

Family reunification in foster care, Pine B, Warsh R, and Malucio A (eds), CWLA inc, 1993, USA.

Lake R, 'Adolescents and Parental Contact', *Adoption & Fostering* 11 (2), 1987.

Mitchell A, *Children in the Middle*, Tavistock, 1985.

'Parent–Child Attachment Concept: Crucial for Permanency Planning', *Social Casework* 63, 1: 46-53, 1982, USA.

Part D, 'Close to Home', *Foster Care*, March 1993.

Proch K, and Howard J, 'Parental Visiting of Children in Foster Care: A study of casework practice', *Social Work* 31, 3: 178-181, 1986, USA.

'Parental Visiting in Foster Care: Law and Practice', *Child Welfare* LXIII, 2: 139-147, 1984, USA.

Rowe J, Hundleby M, and Garrett L, *Child Care Now: A survey of placement patterns*, BAAF, 1989.

Rowe J, Cain H, Hundleby M and Keane A, *Long Term Foster Care*, BAAF/Batsford, 1984.

Thoburn J, *Success and Failure in Permanent Family Placement*, Avebury Gower, 1990.

Trent J, *Homeward Bound: The rehabilitation of children to their birth parents*, Barnardo's New Families Project, 1989.

Triseliotis J, Marsh P, *Prevention and Reunification*, BAAF/Batsford, 1993.

Weinstein E, *The Self-Image of the Foster Child*, Russell Sage Foundation, 1960, USA.